A WILLIAMSON *KIDS CAN!*® BOOK

MAKING

Amazing

ART!

40 activities using the
7 elements of art design

Sandi Henry

Illustrations by Sarah Cole

williamsonbooks™

Nashville, Tennessee

ISBN-13: 978-0-8249-6794-9 (hardcover)
ISBN-13: 978-0-8249-6795-6 (softcover)

Published by Williamson Books
An imprint of Ideals Publications
A Guideposts Company
535 Metroplex Drive, Suite 250
Nashville, Tennessee 37211
www.idealsbooks.com

Library of Congress Cataloging-in-Publication Data
Henry, Sandi, 1951-
    Making amazing art : 40 activities using the 7 elements of art design
/ by Sandi Henry ; illustrated by Sarah Rakitin Cole.
      p. cm. -- (Kids can)
    "A Williamson Kids Can Book."
    Includes index.
    ISBN-13: 978-0-8249-6794-9 (case : alk. paper)
    ISBN-13: 978-0-8249-6795-6 (pbk. : alk. paper)
    ISBN-10: 0-8249-6794-1 (case : alk. paper)
    ISBN-10: 0-8249-6795-X (pbk. : alk. paper)
    1. Handicraft--Juvenile literature. 2. Art--Technique--Juvenile literature. 3. Design--Technique--Juvenile literature. I. Cole, Sarah Rakitin. II. Title.

TT160.H4145 2007
745.5--dc22

                          2006101173

Kids Can!® series editor: Susan Williamson
Project editor: Vicky Congdon
Interior design: Sydney Wright
Cover illustration: Copyright © by Michael Kline
Cover design: Michael Kline

Kaleidoscope Kids®, *Kids Can!*®, *Little Hands*®, *Quick Starts for Kids*®, and *Tales Alive!*® are registered trademarks of Ideals Publications. *Good Times*™, *Quick Starts Tips!*™, and *Little Hands Story Corners*™ are trademarks of Ideals Publications.

Printed and bound in China

10 9 8 7 6 5 4 3 2 1

Dedication

In memory of my brother Tim DeWayne Inman. He lived a life of creative inspiration.

Acknowledgments

My thanks to God for giving me a creative mind and the opportunity to use it in the writing of this book.

Thanks to the great team that used its talents to pull this book together: Susan Williamson for her editorial oversight, Vicky Congdon for her editorial skill in the revision of the text, Sarah Cole for the illustrations, Sydney Wright for the layout and design, and Michael Kline for the cover design.

My thanks to my husband, Terry, for his encouragement and computer assistance, and to my daughter Laura for her patience when I was busy with this book and for her willingness to make artwork examples for me.

Special thanks to all the young artists who contributed the wonderful artwork to this book.

Deepest appreciation to Jessika Henry, Connie Cox, Rex Inman, Louis Torres, Sal Kapunan, Dallas Smart, Tara Belk, Joe Miller, Richard Kaiser, and Sandy Adair, who provided original works of art as well as insight into the artistic process.

Permissions

Contents

Decorative-Line Design, page 12
Matthew, age 9

Shape Hunt, page 42
Kendall, age 13

Tertured-Flowers Bouquet, page 48
Jakob, age 10

Beautiful
Butterfly, page 80
Andrew, age 8

Additive Paper
Sculpture, page 97
Gabriella, age 9

Giant Sunflower,
page 113
Vanessa, age 8

Designing *Amazing* Art!

I've been teaching art for 16 years, and year after year, one of my favorite roles as a teacher is showing young artists how to use the basic concepts of art design to take a piece of art from "That's nice" to "Wow!"

The seven elements of art design — line, shape, texture, color, value, form, and space — are the building blocks that all artists work with to create many different types of art, from drawings and paintings to collage, weaving, and sculpture. Knowing how to apply these concepts will help you achieve certain effects in your own artwork. Let's say you've always wanted to do a realistic drawing of your cat, showing exactly how soft the fur looks. FURRY PET PORTRAIT (see pages 57 and 58) in the Texture chapter will help you do just that! Understanding and practicing the principles of perspective in the Space chapter (see pages 110 to 123), on the other hand, will help you to visually express the concepts of distance and depth in a landscape picture.

Visual Music, page 20
Adam, age 12

To further illustrate these design concepts, you'll find examples of art by famous artists from different styles and periods of art history throughout the book. You'll also hear contemporary artists explain in their own words how they used a particular design element in a piece of art.

You'll find inspiration for your art all around you. Just about everywhere you look, you'll see the elements of line, shape, form, texture, and color in the natural world as well as in the man-made items we use every day. And don't forget the most important tool for making amazing art — your imagination! Using the activities in this book as a guide, experiment with the techniques, and apply the concepts to create original art that's a personal reflection of you. That's what truly "amazing art" is all about!

Sandi Henry

Materials You'll Need

The art materials you'll need are readily available in arts and crafts departments or in art supply stores. If you have trouble finding any items, see RESOURCES, page 124.

Paint

Tempera paint is a water-based paint that is *opaque* (you can't see through it). I recommend the liquid variety in a "premium grade." It has an acrylic medium added to keep it from cracking once it's dry. For the painting projects in this book, you'll need the primary and secondary colors (see pages 59 and 60), along with black and white. You'll learn how to mix them to create a wide range of colors.

Color Explosion,
page 71
Chelsea, age 14

Illustrations and Icons

The activities in this book are illustrated with paintings by my art students. Their artwork is only meant as an inspiration. You'll notice that the step-by-step illustrations sometimes show creating a piece of art that is a little different from the finished piece of student art (a different subject or different colors, for example). There is no one way to create the projects in this book, so please experiment with design elements and techniques to create art that is all yours!

The level of difficulty of each activity is identified with these icons:

🌲 **Simple.** These activities require a minimum of materials and use basic elements of design and art techniques. Perfect for beginning students.

🌲🌲 **Medium challenge level.** Great for students in second to fourth grades.

🌲🌲🌲 **Most challenging.** These activities apply more advanced techniques or design elements that may be slightly more difficult to execute. Recommended for students in fifth, sixth, and seventh grades.

Simple icons in each chapter will remind you at a glance of the design element you're working with:

 Line   Value

 Shape   Form

 Texture   Space

 Color

Watercolor paint is a water-based paint that's *transparent* (you can see through it). A box of eight watercolor paints is perfect for the projects that specify watercolor.

Paintbrushes

It's helpful to own several brushes in different sizes. Flat-ended brushes give you a wide brushstroke. Round-ended brushes are numbered according to thickness. A round number 6 is good to use with watercolor paints; a number 4 works well for painting details.

Paper

Most of the projects specify good-quality paper. Paper comes in different thicknesses, indicated by a weight. White vellum paper (60 lb or heavier) is good choice when you're working with tempera paints. Watercolor paints look best on watercolor paper or other absorbent white paper. Use a thicker weight (90 lb or heavier); it won't wrinkle as much when you paint on it.

Textured-Paper Bird Collage, page 53 Erin, age 13

Pencils

Where a soft lead pencil is specified for drawing, look for a pencil labeled 2B. To get rich, bright colors when working with colored pencils, choose a set with thick, soft leads, such as Prismacolor pencils.

TiPS FOR Art Success

◉ Before starting any messy art project, protect your work surface with old newspaper.

◉ Wear an old shirt to protect your clothes from paint, glue, and other materials.

◉ When painting, keep your paint colors clean. When you are ready to switch to a new color, swish the brush gently in a container of clean water. Wipe it off on a piece of paper towel, and you're ready for the next color! Change the water as needed.

◉ Clean up thoroughly at the end of each project. Set the artwork in a safe place to dry, if necessary. Tightly close all paint containers and thoroughly clean your brushes with mild dish detergent and warm water, and place them on paper towels to dry. Store brushes in a container with the bristles pointing *up*.

Design Element #1

Line

Pick up a piece of paper and a pen or pencil to draw with, and chances are, you'll start by moving the point along to form a *line*. The line is one of the most basic elements of art design. You can use any pointed tool to create one — a pencil, pen, crayon, marker, paintbrush, even a stick in the sand!

The line may sound simple and it's certainly easy to create, but you'll find it's surprisingly expressive. Lines can be thick or thin, light or dark, straight, curvy, jagged or broken, and you can use them to show feelings, ideas, and movement.

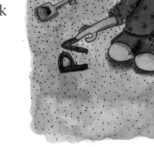

Let's look at the five main types of lines and see how you can use them to create different effects in a piece of artwork. When you repeat any of these types of lines to create a pattern, they're called *decorative lines*.

Vertical lines move up and down so they lead your eye in those directions. They can create a feeling of strength and stability and make certain objects look taller.

Horizontal lines move from side to side. They make objects appear balanced and create feelings of peace and restfulness.

Diagonal lines lean to one side. They can be used to express a feeling of instability or tension. They also express movement.

Zigzag lines are made by connecting diagonal lines. Use them to express action, energy, sound, or just plain confusion!

Curved lines gracefully move and turn. Some curved lines form spirals or circles.

Lines that are used to outline an object or to show the edges of things in a simple way are called *contour lines*.

Just about everywhere you look in the natural world, you'll find lines. They range from teeny-tiny to seemingly endless — just picture a blade of grass or think about the horizon line. Artists learn to look for these natural lines in their surroundings and to use them in their art. You can also see lines in objects that people have created, like skyscrapers, cars, and furniture.

Artists use lines to show rhythm and create movement. In the painting *Rush*, Jessika Henry used short brushstrokes to make colorful curved lines that direct your eyes around the painting.

*"*To see we have to forget the names of the things we are observing."
—Claude Monet, painter

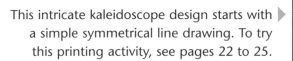

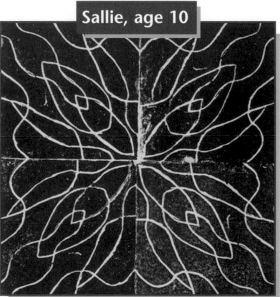

This intricate kaleidoscope design starts with a simple symmetrical line drawing. To try this printing activity, see pages 22 to 25.

Linear Web Design

The morning dew on a spider web reflects the sun and allows us to see the web's beautiful linear design. You can make the lines of a spider-web design magically appear in this crayon-resist painting.

What you need

- Old newspaper to protect your work surface
- White or yellow crayon
- Watercolor paper, 6" x 6" (15 x 15 cm)
- Tape
- Paintbrush
- Container of water
- Blue watercolor paint
- Black permanent marker

et's create it!

1. Use the crayon to make an X that connects the corners of your paper. Make a horizontal and a vertical line that go through the center point of the X.

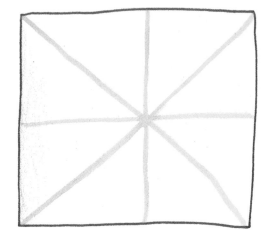

2. Make small connecting lines to complete your spider web design.

3. Tape the corners of your paper to the newspaper-covered work surface. Paint over your paper with water. Paint over the wet paper with blue watercolor paint and watch the spider web appear as the paint sticks to the paper but not to the crayon lines. Let dry.

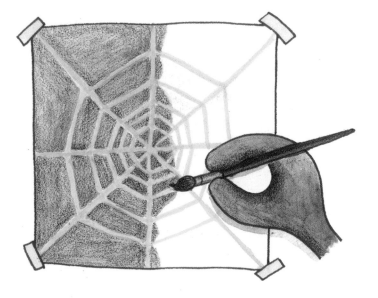

4. Use the marker to draw a spider in the web.

Decorative-Line Design

Quilters often cut apart old quilts and then stitch them back together into pillows or teddy bears. The different fabrics create a variety of patterns. You can create the same effect with a drawing! You begin with contour lines (see page 9) to draw the outline of an object. This artist used a teddy bear, but you can draw something else if you like. Then you add visual interest with a variety of decorative lines (see pages 8 and 9) to represent different fabric designs.

This artist added  further visual interest by turning his bear upside down!

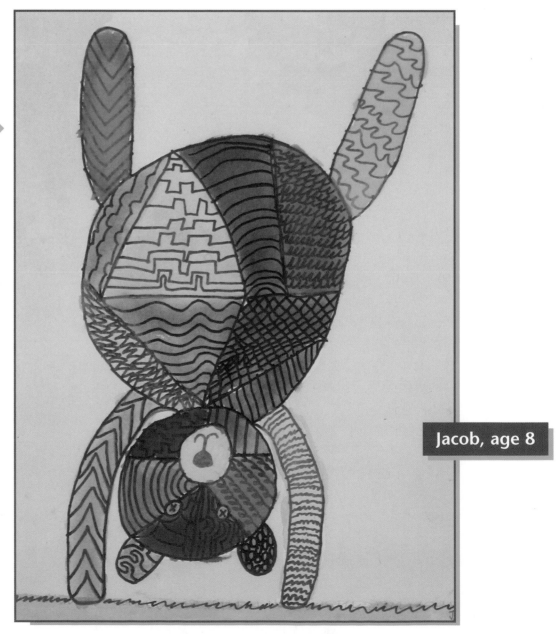

Jacob, age 8

hat you need

- Old newspaper to protect your work surface
- Scrap paper, 9" x 12" (22.5 x 30 cm)
- Pencil
- Markers
- Teddy bear

- Watercolor paper, 12" x 18" (30 x 45 cm)
- Black permanent marker
- Watercolor paints
- Paintbrush
- Container of water and paper towel to clean the paintbrush between colors

et's create it!

1. To find patterns that you like, create a practice sampler full of different decorative lines.

· Fold the scrap paper in half, in half again, and in half again. Open up to reveal eight sections.

Use the markers to make a variety of colorful repeating lines in each section.

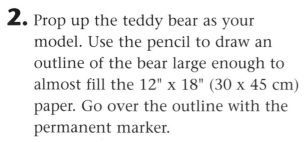

2. Prop up the teddy bear as your model. Use the pencil to draw an outline of the bear large enough to almost fill the 12" x 18" (30 x 45 cm) paper. Go over the outline with the permanent marker.

Divide the bear shape into sections with a few straight, angled lines.

3. With the permanent marker, fill in each area with repeated lines. Use ideas from your practice sampler.

4. Paint over each line-design area with different colors of watercolor paint. (Use enough water to make light colors of paint so the black line design will show through.)

5. Paint the background.

Meet THE Masters

Leonardo da Vinci

Italian painter, sculptor, architect, and engineer
1452–1519

Leonardo da Vinci was one of the greatest artists of all time. What's more, he was also an extremely creative inventor. Da Vinci studied how existing machine parts worked with each other and then combined them in different ways to create new machines that did amazing things that no one had ever imagined possible. He filled notebooks with sketches and detailed descriptions of his inventions. Da Vinci designed submarines, armored tanks, and aircraft hundreds of years before they became a reality.

Da Vinci wrote all his notes in mirror writing, starting on the right-hand side of the page and moving to the left. Some people think that he wrote backwards like this to make it harder for people to read his notes so they wouldn't steal his ideas.

Take a look at da Vinci's drawing of a device he invented called the "aerial screw." Some experts have identified it as the ancestor of the helicopter. Now see MAGICAL MACHINE on the facing page to try *your* hand at inventing a machine!

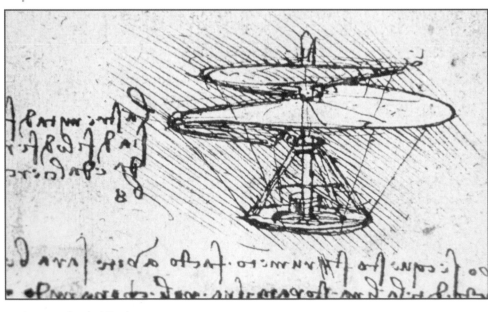

▲ Leonardo da Vinci
Flying machine (aerial screw), ink on paper, probably drawn between 1483 and 1486
From Manuscript B, folio 83 verso.
Bibliothèque de l'Institut de France, Paris, France
Photography: Art Resource, New York

Magical Machine

▲▲ ▲▲

Artists often use contour line drawings (see page 9) to plan for a painting or a piece of sculpture, or the line drawing can be a piece of artwork itself! Make a line drawing of a machine that can do something magical, weird, or wonderful. Give your machine a name and write it backwards, in mirror writing, like Leonardo da Vinci.

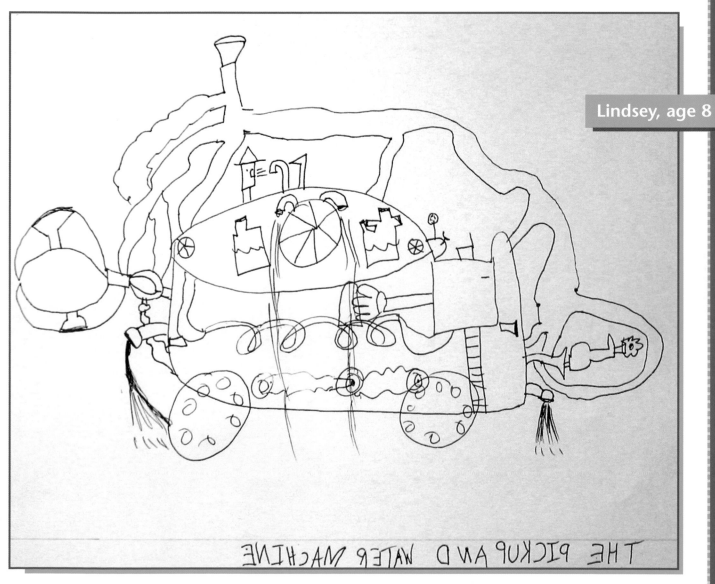

Lindsey, age 8

ƎИIHƆAM ЯƎTAW DИA ꟼUꓘƆIꟼ ƎHT

▲ This artist used mirror writing, just like Leonardo da Vinci did! Hold this page up to the mirror to see what she called her magical machine.

What you need

- Good-quality paper
- Black ink pen
- Mirror (optional)

Let's create it!

1. Imagine yourself as an inventor who has entered a contest to design the most creative magical machine. What would it do? How would it work?

2. Begin your drawing by making a shape outline that represents the base of the machine.

3. Add to your base by drawing gears, pullies, levers, faucets, spouts, conveyer belts, or anything else needed to make your machine work (see GADGET GALLERY at left).

4. Write the name of your machine in mirror writing. (It may be helpful to try writing the name of your machine backwards on a piece of scrap paper first. Hold it up to a mirror to check to make sure you got it right.)

Gallery

Do as Leonardo da Vinci did: borrow parts and gadgets from other machines. Here are some to inspire you!

Grid Drawing

▲ ▲ ▲

Have you ever seen a photo of an object and wanted to reproduce it accurately in a painting or a drawing? Instead of thinking, "But I can't draw a wheelbarrow …" (or whatever the object might be), you can use lines to help you do this!

Use a grid to divide up the image into smaller parts. The sections help you to see — and then to draw — how the edges of shapes join together. By breaking the image down into basic shapes like this, you can easily transfer the image from the photo into the basic shapes of your painting.

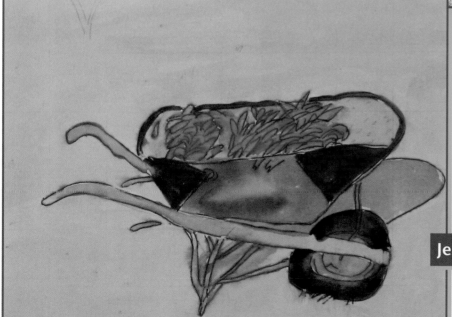

Jessica, age 12

hat you need

- Old newspaper to protect your work surface
- Ruler
- Black ink pen or fine-tip permanent marker
- Picture cut from a magazine or a photocopy of an enlarged photo*
- Good-quality white paper, 9" x 12" (22.5 x 30 cm); use watercolor paper if you intend to paint your picture

- Pencil with eraser
- Colored pencils or watercolor paints
- Paintbrush (if necessary)
- Container of water and paper towel to clean the paintbrush between colors (if necessary)

* Choose a picture of an object, an animal, or a landscape. Pictures without too much detail work best.

et's create it!

1. With the ruler and the pen or marker, make a grid of 1" (2.5 cm) squares over the picture or photo.

2. On the white paper, use the ruler and the pencil to lightly draw a grid of 1" (2.5 cm) squares. Be sure to make the pencil marks *very* light so they can be erased.

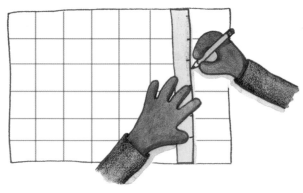

3. Starting in the upper left square of your picture and working to the right, transfer the lines that form the edges of the shapes from each square to the matching section on your pencil-grid paper.

So that you can focus on one small section of the drawing at a time, you might find it helpful to cover the area you're not working on with a blank sheet of paper.

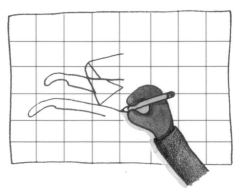

4. Go over your pencil contour drawing with the pen or the fine-tip marker.

5. Carefully erase the pencil grid lines. You now have a contour line drawing of your picture! Add color and details to your picture with colored pencils or watercolor paints.

Enlarge Your Drawing!

It's easy to make a drawing that's bigger than your original picture just by making the pencil grid bigger. For example, if you make a 1" (2.5 cm) grid on your magazine picture, and a 2" (5 cm) grid on your paper, your completed contour drawing will be twice as big!

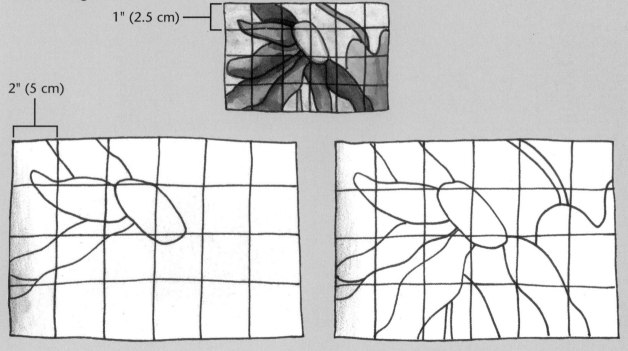

1" (2.5 cm)

2" (5 cm)

Visual Music

Lines can show emotion, movement, and even music! This artist used graceful curving lines to create the impression of soft, soothing music.

Listen to some of your favorite music while you paint, and let your imagination guide your paintbrush.

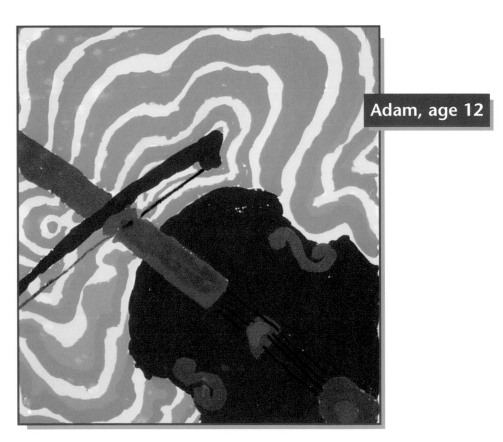

Adam, age 12

 **hat you need**

- ◉ Old newspaper to protect your work surface
- ◉ Stringed instrument (real or a photograph)
- ◉ Pencil
- ◉ Good-quality paper, 12" x 18" (30 x 45 cm)
- ◉ Music tape or CD

- ◉ Paintbrush
- ◉ Tempera paints
- ◉ Container of water and paper towel to clean the paintbrush between colors
- ◉ Black permanent marker
- ◉ Ruler

Let's create it!

1. Set the photo or the instrument about 4' (1.5 m) away from you. Look at it carefully as you draw the contour line of the body of the instrument. Draw the neck as well as the sound hole (details are not necessary at this point).

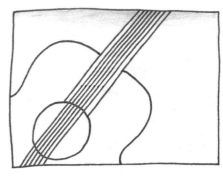

2. Listen to the type of music that you want to illustrate in your painting and draw lines that represent the sounds you hear.

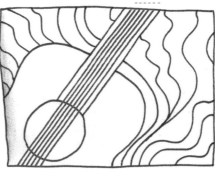

3. Paint your instrument with either realistic colors or unusual expressive colors, depending on the effect you want to create.

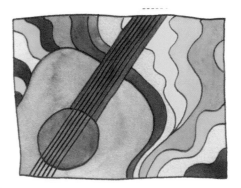

4. Paint the lines of background music with colors that express your idea. You might use bright colors to express loud music, or you might choose less intense colors for soft, soothing music, but it's really up to you and the feelings you want to create.

5. Use the permanent marker and the ruler to add the strings and other details to your instrument.

Meet THE Masters

Georgia O'Keeffe

American painter
1887–1986

Painter Georgia O'Keeffe was very expressive in her use of both line and color. She is particularly famous for her large, detailed portraits of flowers, but she painted other abstract (see page 41) subjects as well. For example, take a look at the painting *Blue and Green Music* at the website of the Art Institute of Chicago (see RESOURCES, page 124). Notice how many different types of lines O'Keeffe used, as well as the colors she chose. How do the lines create the effect of movement? What kind of music does this painting make you think of?

Kaleidoscope Lines

To create a kaleidoscope design, start with a simple symmetrical line drawing. (A *symmetrical* design is one that is exactly the same on both sides of a center line.) When you print your design four times inside a large square, the connecting lines create intricate shapes.

Jessica, age 10

What you need

- Old newspaper to protect your work surface
- Lightweight paper, 6" x 6" (15 x 15 cm)
- Pencil
- Scissors
- Clean Styrofoam trays (from fruits or vegetables only), 2

- Masking tape
- Printing ink in the color of your choice (available at art supply stores)
- Brayer (a small roller for spreading ink; available at art supply stores)
- Good-quality paper, 12" x 12" (30 x 30 cm)

Let's create it!

1. Fold your square of lightweight paper in half to form a triangle. Position the paper as shown. Make a dot on the bottom corner.

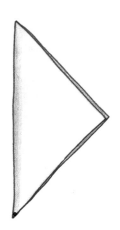

2. Starting at the dot and ending at or near the top corner, draw an interesting design that touches both sides of the paper in several places.

3. Flip your triangle over so the blank side is facing up. Hold it against a sunny window and trace over the design.

4. Open to reveal an interesting symmetrical design.

5. Cut a 6" x 6" (15 x 15 cm) square from one of the Styrofoam trays. Tape your design to the square. Trace over the lines, using enough pressure to make an indentation on the foam.

6. Remove the paper line drawing. Go over the lines in the tray with your pencil so they are fairly deep.

7. Spread a small amount of printing ink in the other Styrofoam tray. Roll the brayer back and forth in the ink to get an even coating on it. Then roll the brayer over the entire 6" (15 cm) square.

8. Look carefully at your inked design to decide which corner should touch the center of your final design. Carefully turn the square over and, with the corner you chose pointing into the center of the paper, place the square in the bottom right corner of the good-quality paper. Press down.

Make a dot on the back of the foam square at the corner that touches the center of the paper.

9. Re-ink your printing square. Place it on another corner of your paper, positioning the printing square so that the dot is in the center. Continue printing until you have filled the remaining two corners.

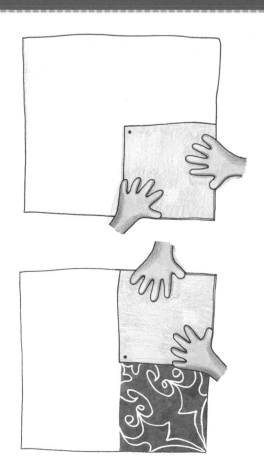

More Art Ideas!

Try creating a different design by repositioning the printing square so that the dot (see step 8) is at the *outside* corners of the large paper each time, instead of in the center.

Use graphite paper (similar to carbon paper; available at art supply stores) to transfer the paper design you created (steps 1 through 4) to the four quarters of a 12" x 12" (30 x 30 cm) piece of good-quality paper. Color the designs created by the connecting lines.

Shape

When you use a continuous line to form an enclosed area, you've created a *shape*. On paper, a shape is a flat enclosed area that can be measured by its height and width.

Geometric shapes have defined edges. They are precise and regular. Man-made objects are often made with geometric shapes.

Here are some simple geometric shapes.

SQUARE	TRIANGLE	RECTANGLE	CIRCLE	OVAL

Combining simple geometric shapes creates complex geometric shapes.

DIAMOND	PARALLELOGRAM	TRAPEZOID	OCTAGON

It might surprise you to see the relationship between geometric shapes, which sounds like math class, and creating a piece of art. But geometric shapes can create a striking visual effect when you repeat them to create patterns, as shown in this quilt.

◀ Even though author Sandi Henry used many colors and patterns of material in this quilt, the repeated geometric shapes bring a sense of orderliness and unity to the piece.

Free-form shapes are irregular and uneven. They can be made with curved lines, straight lines, or a combination of both. And don't forget shapes created from your imagination. You can be as free as you like when you invent your own shapes in your art!

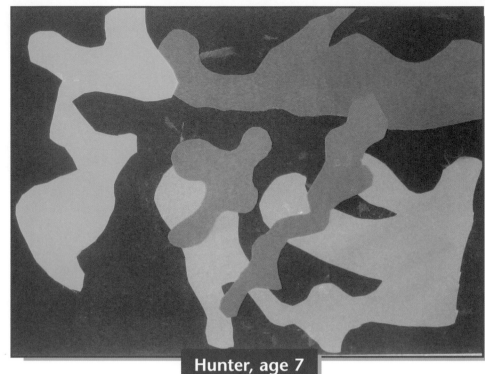

Hunter, age 7

Keep an eye out for free-form shapes in nature. Leaves, flowers, even a puddle of water are a few examples.

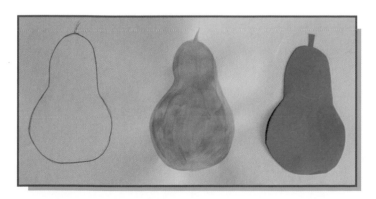

In your art, you can use a simple contour line (see page 9) to show the edges of a shape, or you can create the shape by using a different color or texture to distinguish the space from the space around it.

Shapes can be positive or negative. The main object in a painting is usually the **positive shape** — it has "weight" and stands out against the background. The surrounding background area is considered the **negative shape**. When you use both positive and negative shapes in a thoughtful way, it has a very pleasing effect.

Kassie, age 13

In this drawing, the horses are the positive shapes in the picture. See how they stand out against the negative shape of the background?

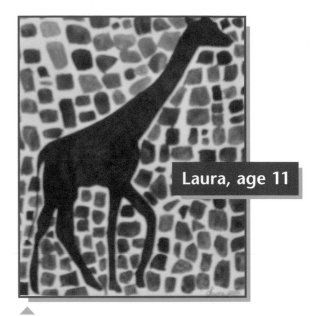

Laura, age 11

Here is an unusual and interesting way to combine positive and negative shapes. What is the effect of having some positive shapes in the background?

Coloring the negative space around the letters instead of the letters themselves makes an intriguing painting. To try this effect, see LETTER & NUMBER SHAPES, pages 40 and 41.

Laura, age 12

Geometric & Free-Form Combo

Here's a fun way to combine geometric and free-form shapes. Create a woven basket made of colorful squares and rectangles. Then fill it with free-form printed apple shapes.

Spencer, age 8

What you need

- Old newspaper to protect your work surface
- Brown construction paper, 6" x 12" (15 x 30 cm)
- Ruler
- Pencil
- Scissors
- Construction paper strips, 1" x 12" (2.5 x 30 cm), 6 in various colors
- Glue
- White construction paper, 12" x 18" (30 x 45 cm)
- Marker
- Tempera paints in red and green
- Paper plates, 2
- Apple
- Knife (for use with adult help)

Let's create it!

1. On the brown paper, measure and draw a horizontal line 1" (2.5 cm) from the bottom as shown. Draw a series of vertical lines 1" (2.5 cm) apart down to the horizontal line as shown.

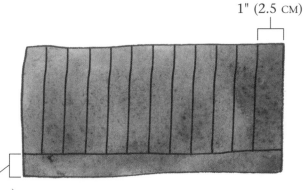

1" (2.5 CM)

1" (2.5 CM)

2. Cut along each vertical line, stopping at the horizontal line each time.

3. Weave each paper strip in and out between the cut strips of brown paper, forming a woven mat. Glue down the ends.

4. Glue the woven section near the bottom of the white construction paper to represent a basket. Use the marker to draw a basket handle.

5. Pour a small amount of red tempera paint onto one paper plate and small amount of green onto the other plate. Spread into a thin layer.

6. Cut the apple in half. Place the cut side into the red paint. Lift the apple and print on the white paper just above the basket. Make three or four more red apple prints.

7. Place the other half of the apple in the green paint and print three or four apples above the basket.

Shape Discovery

Create brand-new shapes when you combine simple geometric shapes. See how many new shapes you can make!

Jackson, age 6

What you need

- Old newspaper to protect your work surface
- Construction-paper squares, 2" x 2" (5 x 5 cm), 20
- Construction-paper equilateral triangles*, 2" (5 cm), 20
- Construction paper, 12" x 18" (30 x 45 cm)
- Glue stick

* In an equilateral triangle, all three sides are the same size.

Let's create it!

1. Place squares and triangles side by side on the 12" x 18" (30 x 45 cm) paper to create different shapes. Try combining them in different ways to make new and unusual shapes.

2. When you are pleased with your arrangement of shapes, glue them in place. How many new shapes did you make?

Tangram Art Puzzle

Ready to try your hand at a more challenging activity using geometric shapes? A *tangram* is an ancient Chinese puzzle consisting of seven geometric shapes cut from a square. You can arrange the seven pieces in various ways to make countless silhouette shapes.

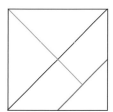

On a 6" x 6" (15 x 15 cm) square of sturdy paper, use a ruler and colored pencils to draw lines in this order: blue, red, and green.

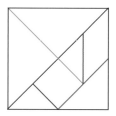

Add the two purple lines as shown.

Carefully cut out the pieces. Try making the animal shapes shown here.

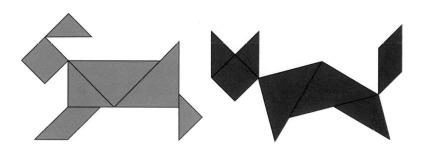

Then try creating some tangrams of your own!

Henri Matisse

French painter and collage artist
1869–1954

Henri Matisse discovered his interest and talent in art when he was 21 years old. While he was recovering from a serious illness, his mother brought him a paint set. From that day on, Matisse knew he had found his gift. He spent the rest of his life as an artist and painted many pictures during his career.

Toward the end of his life, Matisse began to make art in a different way. He painted paper with beautiful colors and then cut simple shapes from the paper. He carefully arranged the shapes to create large picture collages. He called this style of art "cutouts." Some of his cutouts are big enough to cover an entire wall, while others are the size of this page.

▲ Henri Matisse
Snow Flowers, 1951
Watercolor and gouache on cut and pasted papers; 68½" x 31¾" (174 x 80.6 cm)
The Metropolitan Museum of Art, Jacques and Natasha Gelman Collection, 1998 (1999.383.46)
Photograph © 2004 The Metropolitan Museum of Art
© 2007 Succession H. Matisse, Paris/Artists Rights Society (ARS), New York

Cutout Collage

▲▲

Make a cutout collage just as Henri Matisse did. Cut free-form shapes out of colored construction paper. Use them to create an arrangement that you like, then glue them to a background of a contrasting color.

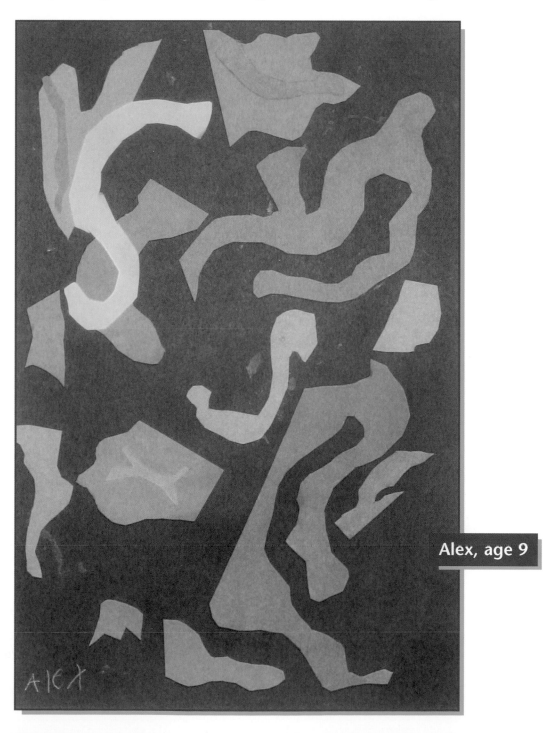

Alex, age 9

What you need

- Old newspaper to protect your work surface
- Scissors
- Construction paper in a variety of colors that go well together
- Glue stick

Let's create it!

1. Cut several free-form shapes from different colors of construction paper. No need to draw the shapes first; just hold a sheet of paper with one hand and start cutting. As you cut, keep turning your paper until you have made an interesting shape.

2. Choose a piece of paper in a contrasting color for the background. Arrange your shapes on the paper. Experiment with overlapping some and placing others by themselves. When you have an arrangement you like, glue the shapes in place.

Capture Shadow Shapes

Discover interesting free-form shapes just by looking at the shadows of natural objects, such as the leaves or blossoms of a plant. Position a sketch pad on the ground so the shadows fall on it. Use a black felt-tipped marker to draw the outline, or contour lines, of the shapes. Then fill in the shapes with a black or colored marker.

Stencil Shapes

One simple stencil can create an amazing design when you use it to make repeating shapes. Explore the new shapes you can create by overlapping your stencil.

Abigail, age 10

What you need

- ☉ Old newspaper to protect your work surface
- ☉ Construction paper, 6" x 6" (15 x 15 cm)
- ☉ Scissors
- ☉ Chalk in a variety of colors
- ☉ Light-colored construction paper, 12" x 18" (30 x 45 cm)
- ☉ Acrylic spray (available at art supply stores; for use with adult help in a well-ventilated area)

1. To create a shape stencil, fold the 6" x 6" (15 x 15 cm) paper in half and cut out a free-form shape along the folded edge. Open the shape and lay it flat. Open the folded paper with the hole in it and lay it flat next to your cut shape. You now have two shapes.

The *negative shape* is the area around the hole, which is also a shape.

The *positive shape* is the shape itself.

2. Draw a line of colored chalk along the outside edge of the positive shape. Place the stencil on the light-colored paper, chalk side up. Holding the stencil in place, use your finger to rub the chalk from the stencil onto the surface of the paper. The streaks of chalk will radiate away from the shape.

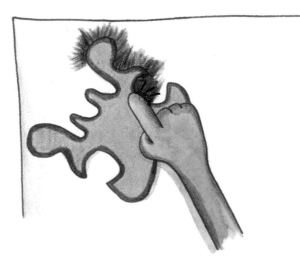

3. Rechalk the outside edge of the positive shape. Position your shape on another area of your paper. Rub the chalk from the stencil to the paper.

Repeat the process several times over the surface of your paper. You may want to overlap some of the shapes, creating new and interesting shapes.

4. Use a different color of chalk to make a line along the edge of the hole of the negative shape. Place the shape on the paper. Holding it in place, rub the chalk from the stencil shape onto the paper. The streaks of chalk will radiate toward the center of the hole.

Repeat this process several times, repositioning the shape each time.

5. Spray the finished artwork with acrylic spray.

Geometric Shape Magic!

Rub chalk from the edges of geometric shapes onto black paper. Spray the finished artwork with acrylic spray.

Brittney, age 7

Letter & Number Shapes

Positive and negative shapes (see page 28) can work together in an intriguing way to create visual interest in a piece of artwork. By coloring the positive and negative shapes in a new way, you can create an interesting piece of abstract art that tells the viewers something about you!

Laura, age 12

 hat you need

- ☺ Old newspaper to protect your work surface
- ☺ Pencil
- ☺ Ruler
- ☺ Good-quality light-colored paper, 8½" x 11" (21 x 27.5 cm)
- ☺ Crayon or marker in the color of your choice

Let's create it!

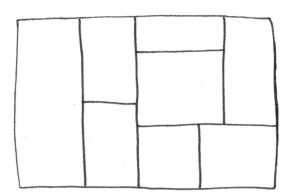

1. Draw horizontal and vertical lines to divide your paper with into various-sized squares and rectangles. Create a total of 7 to 11 sections.

2. Lightly write the letters of your name and the numbers for the year you were born with the pencil so that each letter or number fits into a shape by touching at least two sides. It is important that your pencil marks are very light in case you need to erase to make adjustments to the shape.

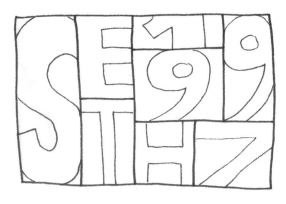

3. The letters and the numbers are the positive shapes; the shapes created between the letters and numbers are the negative shapes. Color either the positive shape or the negative shape within each square or rectangle to make a cool abstract art design.

WHAT'S Abstract?

In a piece of abstract art, you don't depict a realistic image of something. You might change, or *abstract*, a recognizable subject, and represent it in an unusual way. Or you might simply use lines, shapes, and colors to create a design or pattern.

Shape Hunt

Use a viewfinder to reveal interesting abstract shapes within a large picture. Then enlarge the small area in the viewfinder to create an abstract composition. Show your artwork along with the original magazine picture to a friend and see if he or she can pick out the portion that you enlarged!

Kendall, age 13

hat you need

- Old newspaper to protect your work surface
- Good-quality paper, 8" x 8" (20 x 20 cm), 2
- Ruler
- Pencil

- Scissors
- Old magazines
- Tape
- Markers, crayons, or colored pencils

Let's create it!

1. Fold one piece of paper in half. Measure, mark, and cut a 1" x 2" (2.5 x 5 cm) rectangle on the fold. Open to reveal a 2" (5 cm) square hole. This is your viewfinder.

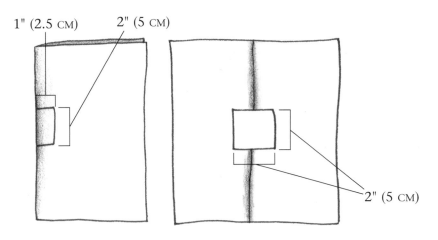

1" (2.5 CM)   2" (5 CM)

2" (5 CM)

2. Move the viewfinder over various magazine pictures to find a combination of shapes that you like. When you do, tape the viewfinder in place.

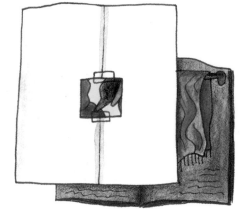

3. Look at the outline of each shape shown inside the viewfinder. Draw a larger version of those shapes on the other piece of paper.

4. Color your abstract artwork with markers, crayons, or colored pencils.

Texture

Texture is the element of art that creates the look and feel of an object's outside surface. When you see something with an interesting texture, what is the first thing you want to do? Touch it, of course! We experience texture with our sense of touch but also with our sense of sight.

▲
Author Sandi Henry used small smooth river rocks to create a textured mosaic design on one wall of her house. Can you pick out the flowers?

Tactile texture is actual surface texture that can be touched. These textures can range from the rough gritty feel of sandpaper to the smooth feel of marble.

You'll find a wide variety of tactile textures in nature as well as in man-made objects. Imagine running your fingers over a cat's fur, the bark of a tree, or the surface of a rock. Now think of the way a book, a rug, or the bottom of a sneaker feels — these man-made objects all have different textures, too.

Collage is one type of artwork that uses tactile texture to add visual interest. This artist combined pieces of felt, wallpaper, fabric, magazine pictures, and yarn to create the cat image at right.

Becky, age 9

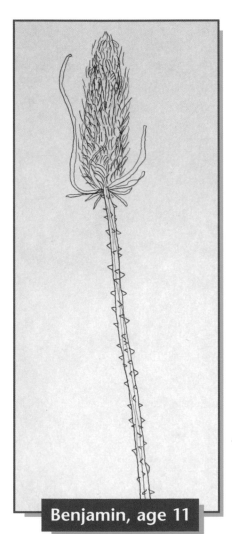

Benjamin, age 11

An artist can also represent texture with repeated patterns of dots, lines, and shapes. To create this **visual texture**, you draw a surface so it looks the way it would feel if you touched it. Some textures are soft and smooth; others are rough and scratchy. Carefully observing and feeling actual textures can help you represent them artistically on a two-dimensional surface. To try a very detailed drawing of an animal's fur, see FURRY PET PORTRAIT on pages 57 and 58.

◄ Many artists carry sketchbooks with them so they can record the interesting details they observe in the natural world, such as the different textures on this delicate seed stalk.

Texture Rubbing

exture rubbings are a cool way to show the bumps, grooves, lines, and other patterns on the surface of a textured item. Use this method of coloring your drawing to add interesting visual texture to your artwork.

What you need

- Old newspaper to protect your work surface
- Pencil
- Lightweight paper, 9" x 12" (22.5 x 30 cm)

- Textured items, such as a burlap bag, coarse sandpaper, a plastic netted orange or onion sack, and coins
- Texture plates* (optional)
- Crayons

* Texture plates are plastic squares that come in a variety of textured surfaces and are available at art supply stores (or see RESOURCES, page 124). This artist used a texture plate to make the concentric circles in the sky, but you could also experiment with different household objects to create a similar effect.

Let's create it!

1. With the pencil, make a simple drawing, without much detail, on the lightweight paper.

2. Place a textured item or texture plate under your drawing and rub the side of a crayon over a portion of your picture to transfer the texture.

3. Place a different texture item under your picture and transfer this texture to another area of your drawing.

4. Fill all the areas of your picture with texture, even the background.

More Art Ideas!

You can make rubbings of all kinds of things! Try leaves and tree bark, or an automobile license plate. How about a collection of rubbings of all the different designs for each state found on U.S. quarters?

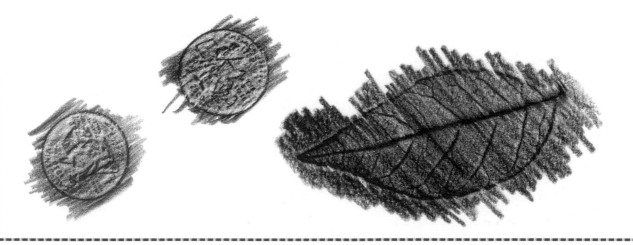

Textured-Flowers Bouquet

Pictures that show texture in magazines are a form of visual texture. In other words, if you actually touched the picture with your hands, you would feel only the smooth surface of the paper. Yet you know the surface texture is there because you experience it with your eyes. Use visual texture from magazine images to create a vase of flowers in an unusual way.

Abigail, age 10

 **hat you need**

- ❂ Old newspaper to protect your work surface
- ❂ Old magazines
- ❂ Scissors
- ❂ Good-quality paper, 9" x 12" (22.5 x 30 cm) and 12" x 18" (30 x 45 cm)
- ❂ Glue stick
- ❂ Green marker

Let's create it!

1. Look through the magazines and cut out pictures that illustrate different textures, particularly textures that could represent flowers. Set them aside.

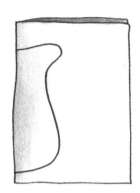
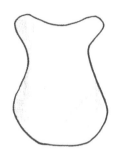

2. Fold the smaller piece of paper in half. Draw half of a vase shape on the paper fold. Cut out the shape and unfold it.

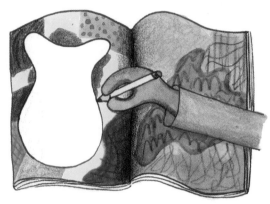

3. Place the vase shape over a magazine photo that shows an interesting texture and trace around it. Cut out the shape. Glue the vase shape on the bottom third of the larger piece of paper.

4. Cut several flower shapes out of the magazine pictures. Arrange the flower shapes above the vase in a pleasing arrangement. Glue in place.

5. With the green marker, draw stems from the flowers to the vase. Cut leaf shapes from magazine pictures and glue them in place along the stems, if you like.

3-D Texture Tapestry

Weaving is an excellent example of an art form where the texture is one of the most important characteristics. Using a simple handmade loom, weave a tapestry that has texture you can see *and* feel. Then add objects for additional three-dimensional texture.

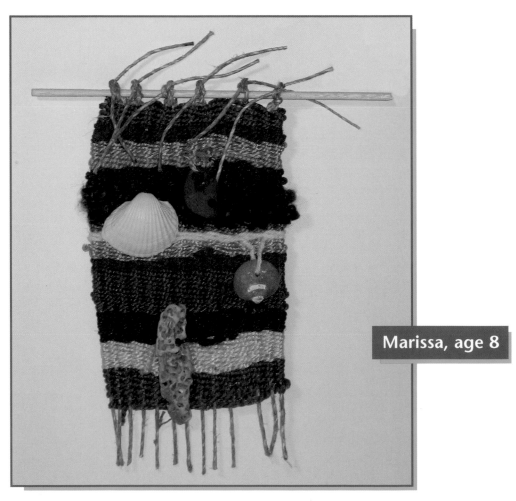

Marissa, age 8

What you need

- Scissors
- Cardboard, 6" x 9" (15 x 22.5 cm)
- Ruler
- Tape
- Ball of string

- Yarns in different textures, such as shiny, fuzzy, or nubby
- Darning needle (large needle with a large eye)
- Buttons, shells, and other 3-D items, with predrilled holes, for weaving to tapestry (optional)
- Wooden dowel (optional)

Let's create it!

1. To make a loom, cut short slits along the top and bottom of the cardboard rectangle ¼ inch (5 mm) apart.

2. Tape the end of the string to the back side of your loom. "Warp" the loom by wrapping the string around and around the loom, through the slits at the top and the bottom as shown. Tape the other end on the back side.

3. Cut a piece of yarn approximately 2' (60 cm) long. Tie one end onto the first warp string and thread the other end through the eye of the darning needle. Begin weaving over and under the warp strings.

When you have woven the yarn all the way across your loom, turn and go back the other way, now going over and under the *opposite* warp strings to create the "weft."

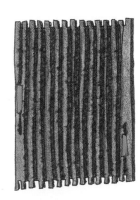

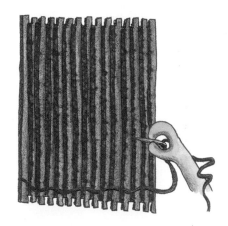

4. Continue weaving back and forth until your yarn gets too short. At this point, tie another piece of yarn to the first one, thread the new piece of yarn onto the needle, and continue weaving.

If possible, add the new piece of yarn toward the center of your weaving rather than at the edges. This way, the ends can be pushed through to the back where they won't be seen.

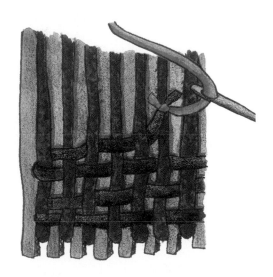

5. To add even more texture as well as variety, experiment with adding buttons or shells with holes in them as you weave by stringing them onto the yarn as shown.

6. When your tapestry is as long as you want it, cut the warp strings in the middle on the back side of the loom.

7. On the top edge, tie the first warp string to the one next to it and knot them. Continue until all strings are knotted. Repeat along the bottom edge. To attach a dowel for hanging as shown in the finished tapestry, tie the warp strings along the top edge around the dowel.

Through the Artist's Eyes

"The Blue Ridge Mountains, which surround my North Carolina home, have been a continuing source of artistic inspiration for me. Working with a drawing of a photo behind my loom, I recreate the picture in my woven art, expressing the ever-changing nuances of light and color I see in these mountains through subtle blending of fibers, color tones, and visual textures."

Blue Ridge Mountain Moonlight
Sandy Adair

Textured-Paper
Bird Collage

▲▲▲

Create unique paper by painting patterns and textures on it.
Then cut shapes from it to create a colorful collage bird.

Erin, age 13

Laura, age 12

What you need

- Old newspaper to protect your work surface
- Tape
- Watercolor paper, 12" x 18" (30 x 45 cm), 2
- Large flat paintbrush
- Container of water
- Watercolor paints
- Paper towel
- Bird pictures (for reference)
- Drawing paper, 12" x 19" (12 x 47.5 cm)
- Pencil
- Small paintbrush for creating texture
- Items to create texture, such a comb, sponge, toothpick, or feather
- Tracing paper
- Scissors
- Glue

Let's create it!

1. Tape down the corners of the watercolor paper to the covered work surface. Use the large paintbrush to wet the entire paper with water.

2. Create a daytime sky with blue watercolor paint, or a colorful sunset sky by using red, orange, and yellow. Make clouds by using a bunched-up paper towel to blot the paint from the still-wet sky. Let dry.

3. Look at a bird picture for reference, and on the drawing paper, draw the contour lines (see page 9) of a bird on a branch or in another natural environment. Set aside.

4. Think about where you might want to use various colors and textures in your collage and paint portions of your other piece of watercolor paper accordingly.

For example, if you want your bird to have a blue body, you can paint a section of the paper with different shades of blue and then use a old comb to create texture that resembles feathers.

For the tree branch, try painting a tan base and then sponging on an overlay of brown paint. Let dry.

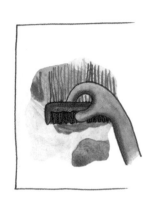
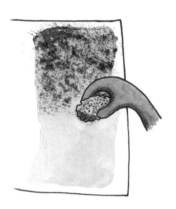

5. Place the tracing paper over your bird drawing and trace the outline. Cut a section of the bird out of the tracing paper. Lay this tracing-paper shape over an area of the painted texture paper and trace around it; cut out that piece.

TRACE AROUND WING SHAPE

6. Glue the cut piece of painted texture paper to the appropriate place on your drawing.

Cut and add more parts until your collage bird is complete.

Meet THE Masters

Albrecht Dürer

German painter and woodcut artist
1471–1528

Albrecht Dürer was one of the greatest artists of his time. Born in 1471 in Nuremberg, Germany, he was one of 18 children. His father was a goldsmith and trained his son in the goldsmith trade at an early age. At the age of 13, however, Dürer drew a self-portrait that clearly showed his talent for drawing, and he decided to pursue a career as a painter instead. He worked as a portrait painter, painting portraits of rich and famous people. He also made woodcuts and watercolor paintings. Texture and details were always an important aspect of Dürer's work. He became known as the master of detail.

Dürer carefully observed live rabbits before making this watercolor painting. He painted hundreds of fine lines close together to create visual texture of soft fur. He wanted to show how the hare would feel if you could really touch it. Do you think he did a good job?

▲ Albrecht Dürer
The Young Hare, 1502
Watercolor and gouache on paper
10" x 9" (25 x 22.5 cm)
Albertina, Vienna, Austria

Furry Pet Portrait

Marissa, age 8

Animals are fun to draw, and they're a great way to practice creating visual texture. Try your hand at creating the textured look of soft animal fur by drawing a portrait of your pet or favorite animal.

 hat you need

⊚ Pet (for model) or close-up photo of an interesting-looking animal
⊚ White paper
⊚ Pencil

 et's create it!

1. Carefully observe an animal such as your pet or study the photo. Draw the contour lines (see page 9) to create an outline of the animal's body.

2. Look closely at the animal's fur. Are the individual hairs long or short? Are they straight, wavy, or very curly? Use repeated lines to represent the texture of the fur.

Meet THE *Masters*

Meret Oppenheim

Swiss (German-born) artist and photographer
1913–1985

Meret Oppenheim was part of a group of artists who made very nontraditional art in the 1930s. She is best known for a piece of sculpture she created called *Object*, a sculpture of a cup, saucer, and spoon. Sounds pretty ordinary, doesn't it? But wait until you see it — the three objects are covered with fur! Take a look at this piece of art online at the website of the Museum of Modern Art in New York (see RESOURCES, page 124) and see if you don't agree that this unusual use of texture makes this ordinary item quite extraordinary! The soft, smooth texture makes you want to reach out and touch it. Why do you think this artist experimented with these materials in this way?

Color

Artists use the design element of *color* in several different ways. Color can show the actual true color of an object, it can also express an emotion or an idea or create a mood, it can even give the feeling of temperature. Color is the design element that often makes the first impression on the viewer, so learning to use color effectively can have a big impact on your artwork.

Jakob, age 10

▲ To explore dramatic uses of color in your artwork, see COLOR EXPLOSION, pages 71 and 72.

primary colors

secondary colors

primary + primary = secondary

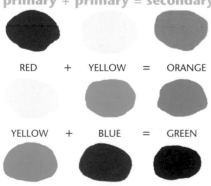

RED	+	YELLOW	=	ORANGE
YELLOW	+	BLUE	=	GREEN
BLUE	+	RED	=	VIOLET

Red, yellow, and blue are **primary colors**.

Primary means first. Each primary color is a pure color that is not created by mixing other colors together. Primary colors are bright and bold and really stand out in your artwork.

The **secondary colors** are orange, green and violet.

Secondary colors are created by mixing two primary colors together. The secondary colors are not as vivid as the primary colors because they are a mixture.

The *color wheel* is a handy tool used by artists to help choose and combine colors for their artwork. It shows at a glance how all the colors are related to one another. The solid black lines connect the primary colors and the dashed lines connect the secondary colors.

Mixing a primary color with a neighboring secondary color creates an **intermediate color**. The names of the intermediate colors are easy to remember — each one tells you what two colors were used to make it.

Placing the colors in a circle called the color wheel shows you how they are related.

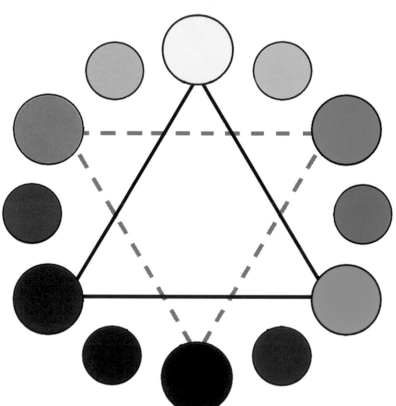

intermediate colors

YELLOW-GREEN   BLUE-GREEN   BLUE-VIOLET   RED-VIOLET   RED-ORANGE   YELLOW-ORANGE

Warm and cool colors can give an impression of temperature. They can also appear to move forward or back in a piece of art.

Cool colors range from yellow-green to violet on the color wheel. They remind us of cool seasons and of water and sky. Cool colors seem to recede or move back when used in a painting.

Warm colors range from yellow to red-violet. They remind us of sunlight, fire and heat. They appear to advance or come toward the viewer in a painting.

Complementary colors are across from each other on the color wheel. These colors are as different from one another as they can be. When you use them side by side in your artwork, they create a strong impact. The primary and secondary colors opposite each other on the color wheel are the colors most often used as complementary pairs.

complementary colors

Intermediate colors have complements as well, however, and you can also find these intermediate color complements by looking at the color wheel. For example, point to yellow-green on the color wheel on page 60. Move your finger directly across the wheel to find its complement — red-violet.

When a color is mixed with a little bit of its complementary color, it lowers the intensity of the original color and makes it appear dull.

Mixing two complementary colors in equal amounts results in a gray. Grays made from complementary colors are richer looking than grays made from mixing black and white.

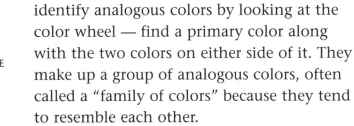

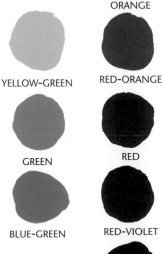
ORANGE

YELLOW-GREEN   RED-ORANGE

GREEN   RED

BLUE-GREEN   RED-VIOLET

VIOLET

Analogous colors are a group of colors that show a likeness to each other. It's easy to identify analogous colors by looking at the color wheel — find a primary color along with the two colors on either side of it. They make up a group of analogous colors, often called a "family of colors" because they tend to resemble each other.

 Here are two groups of analogous colors. Can you find them on the color wheel?

Secondary-Color Surprise

▲

Overlap red, yellow, and blue tissue-paper shapes.
The result? Six colors instead of three! When you mix two of the
primary colors (red, yellow, or blue), you create a secondary color.

Brittany, age 6

What you need

- Old newspaper to protect your work surface
- Tissue paper in red, yellow, and blue
- Shallow container
- Glue
- Water
- Spoon
- White construction paper, 9" x 12" (22.5 x 30 cm)
- Paintbrush
- Container of water and paper towel to clean the paintbrush between glue coats

Let's create it!

1. Tear the tissue paper into medium-sized pieces; set aside. In the shallow container, mix equal parts of glue and water together.

2. Place five or six pieces of yellow tissue paper on the construction paper. Paint over them with the glue mixture. Rinse and wipe the paintbrush.

3. Place blue tissue-paper pieces on the paper so that some of them overlap the yellow pieces. Paint over the blue pieces with the glue mixture and watch green shapes magically appear! Rinse and wipe the paintbrush.

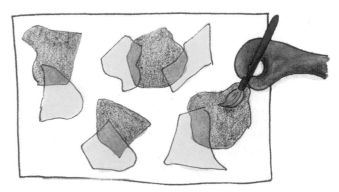

4. Place red tissue-paper pieces on the paper so that parts of the red pieces overlap some yellow or blue pieces. Paint with glue mixture. What new colors do you see?

Warm & Cool Ocean Scene

Use the cool colors (see page 60) ranging from yellow-green to violet on the color wheel to color the water in the background of your picture. Then use warm colors ranging from yellow to red-violet for the fish. See how warm colors pop out as the cool background colors recede?

Becky, age 10

What you need

- Old newspaper to protect your work surface
- Ruler
- Pencil
- Good-quality white paper, 9" x 12" (22.5 x 30 cm), 2
- Scissors
- Crayons or markers

Let's create it!

1. Use the ruler and pencil to measure and mark 1" (2.5 cm) increments around the edges of your paper. Using the ruler, connect the marks with horizontal and vertical lines to create a grid.

1" (2.5 CM)

1" (2.5 CM)

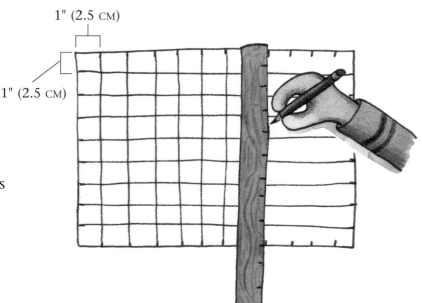

2. On the other piece of paper, draw three to five fish shapes. Cut them out.

3. Position the fish on your grid paper and trace around them as shown. Remove the fish-shape pattern pieces.

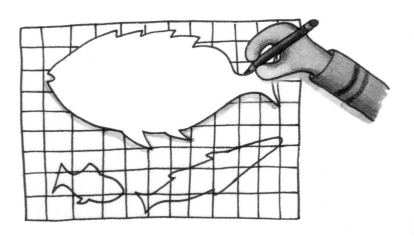

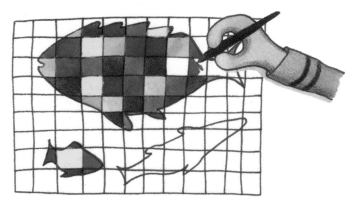

4. Use the crayons or markers to color the outlined fish shapes with warm colors (see page 60). The lines on the grid show you where to change colors.

5. Color the remaining shapes with cool colors (see page 60).

Use One Group of Colors

Kassie, age 13

Discover the effect of using only cool colors or only warm colors by painting a landscape or seascape as shown here. Both of these paintings were drawn and colored with watercolor pencils (available at art supply stores). To achieve this softened look, brush over your finished picture with a paintbrush dipped in water to blend the pencil marks.

Compare the very different moods of these two drawings, one created with only warm colors and the other with only cool colors.

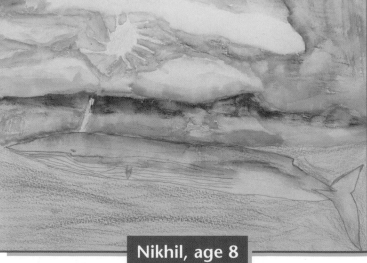

Nikhil, age 8

Complementary-Color Puzzle Design

Complementary colors (see page 61) are as different as two colors can be! When you place them next to each other in a piece of artwork, they really stand out. Cut and glue shapes of complementary colors to make a striking abstract design.

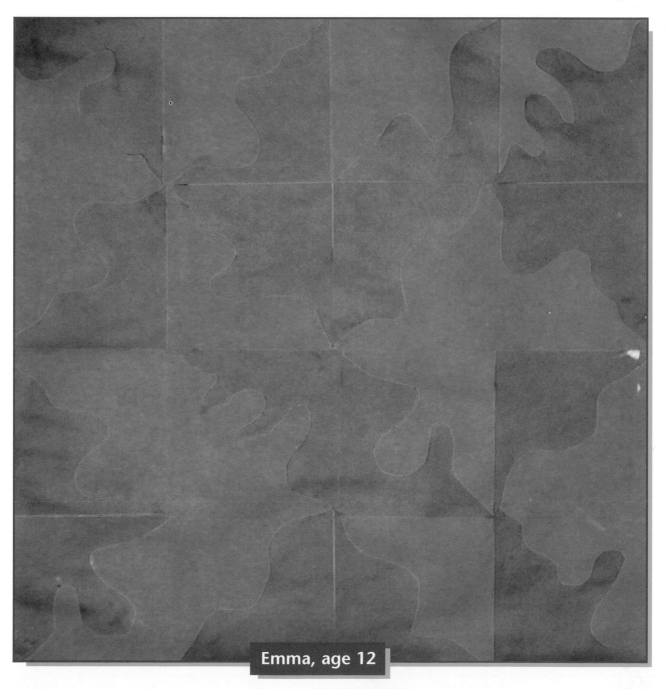

Emma, age 12

hat you need

- Old newspaper to protect your work surface
- Ruler
- Pencil
- Construction paper, 12" (30 cm) square
- Construction paper in a complementary color, 6" x 12" (15 x 30 cm)
- Scissors
- Glue

et's create it!

1. Use the ruler and pencil to mark off every 3" (7.5 cm) around the edges of both pieces of paper. Connect the lines to form a grid.

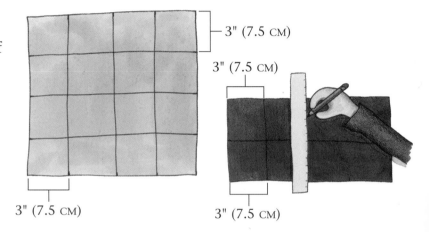

3" (7.5 CM)

3" (7.5 CM)

3" (7.5 CM)

3" (7.5 CM)

2. Cut along the grid lines of the smaller piece of construction paper to create eight 3" (7.5 cm) squares.

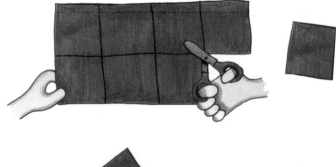

3. Across each of the small squares, cut an interesting diagonal line from corner to corner.

4. Place each triangular shape on the grid to create an abstract design. Rearrange pieces until you are satisfied with your design. Glue in place.

More Art Ideas!

From a piece of 6" x 6" (15 x 15 cm) construction paper, cut strips in interesting shapes. Glue the cut pieces in order onto a piece of 6" x 9" (15 x 22.5 cm) construction paper that's the complementary color, leaving spaces between each strip.

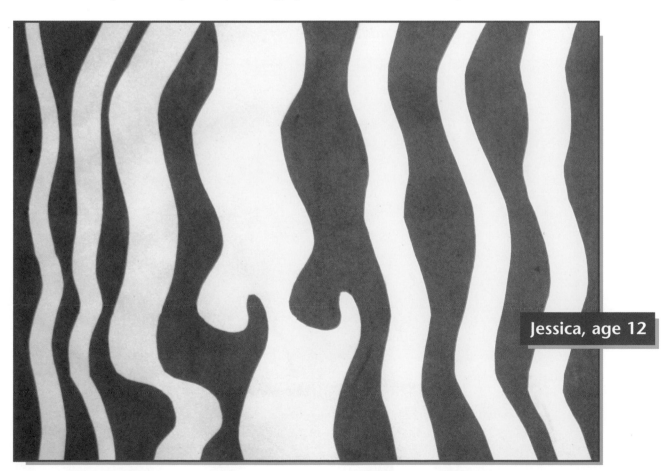

Jessica, age 12

*M*eet THE *M*asters

Robert Delaunay

French painter
1885–1941

Robert Delaunay (RO-bear DEH-law-nay) was born in 1885 in Paris. At the age of 19, he began painting. His artwork was greatly influenced by the Cubist painters of the time. In Cubism, artists depicted objects as if broken apart and then reassembled, so that when you look at the flat surface of the painting, you see several sides of the objects simultaneously. To see an example of a Cubist painting, visit the website of the Art Institute of Chicago (see RESOURCES, page 124) and take a look at *Untitled (Man with Moustache, Buttoned Vest, and Pipe, Seated in an Armchair)*, painted by Pablo Picasso in 1915. Can you pick out all the items in the title?

Inspired by the sun and colors of nature, Delaunay sought to capture the sense of rhythm and motion in color. He once said, "Light in nature creates the movements in colors." In the 1930s, Delaunay began a series of paintings called *Rhythms of Circular Forms*. These paintings (one is shown below) were filled with circular shapes divided into areas of contrasting colors. He continued making art in this way until he died in 1941.

▲ Robert Delaunay
Circular Forms (Formes circulaires), 1930
Oil on canvas, 128.9 x 194.9 cm (50¾ x 76¾ inches)
Solomon R. Guggenheim Museum, New York
49.1184
© L & M SERVICES B.V. Amsterdam 20061116

Color Explosion

Create a colorful abstract painting in the style of Robert Delaunay. Divide circular shapes into different-sized segments and paint them with mixtures of colors that show up well next to each other. For the best effect, take your time choosing the colors and deciding where they will go. Refer to the color wheel on page 60 for help with the color relationships.

Chelsea, age 14

What you need

- Old newspaper to protect your work surface
- Pencil
- Compass or small round objects like jar lids or cups
- Good-quality white paper, 12" x 18" (30 x 45 cm)
- Ruler
- Tempera paints
- Paintbrush
- Container of water and paper towel to clean the paintbrush between colors
- Paper plates

[L]et's create it!

1. Draw several circular shapes on your paper with a compass or by tracing round objects. Make some circles within other circles. Make a few circles that overlap. Use the ruler to divide your shapes into smaller sections.

2. Begin by painting several areas throughout your design with the bright, bold primary colors — red, yellow, and blue. Repeating colors throughout your painting will create a sense of balance and unity.

3. Choose a secondary color, and repeat it in a few places throughout your painting. Using this color next to its color complement will create an appealing effect.

4. Continue painting with the remaining secondary colors.

Using the color wheel on page 60, create intermediate colors by mixing a primary color with a neighboring secondary color.

Create lighter and darker colors by mixing in either a little black or white paint.

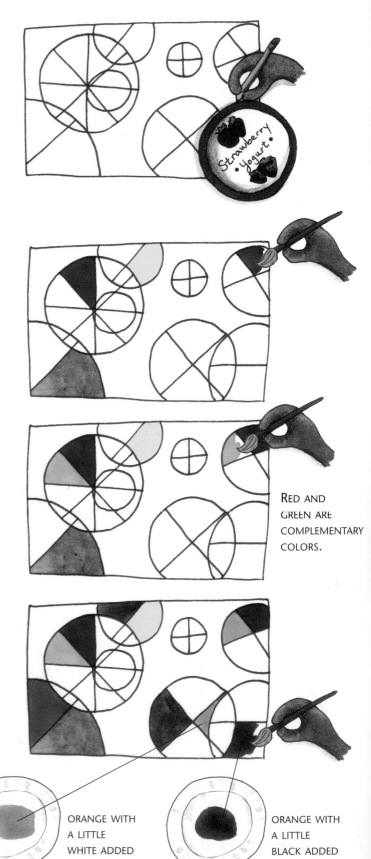

RED AND GREEN ARE COMPLEMENTARY COLORS.

ORANGE WITH A LITTLE WHITE ADDED

ORANGE WITH A LITTLE BLACK ADDED

Analogous-Color Puzzle

▲ ▲ ▲

Analogous colors are a group of colors that show a likeness to each other because they all have one color in common (see page 61). When you use analogous colors together, they create a pleasing sense of color harmony. Notice how the design elements of line (see pages 8 and 9) and shape (see pages 26 to 28) work with the elements of color in this piece of art.

Using the color wheel on page 60, choose a family of analogous colors to create the pieces for your puzzle painting.

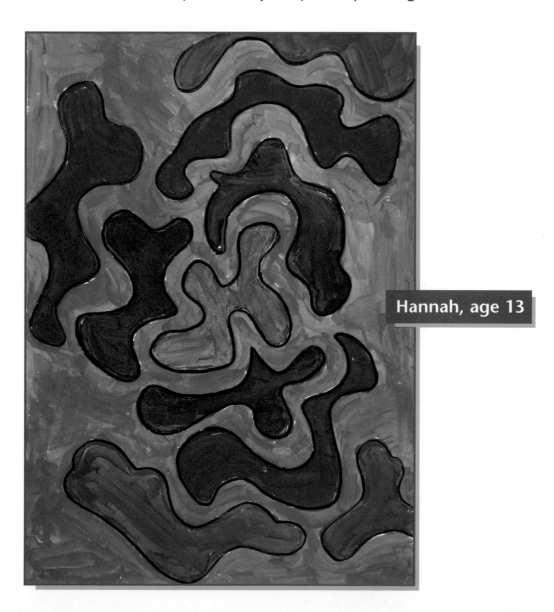

Hannah, age 13

hat you need

- Old newspaper to protect your work surface
- Good-quality white paper, 9" x 12" (22.5 x 30 cm)
- Pencil
- Tempera paints
- Paintbrush
- Paper plates, 5
- Container of water and paper towel to clean the paintbrush between colors
- Black permanent marker

et's create it!

1. In the center of the paper, draw a free-form shape similar to a puzzle piece.

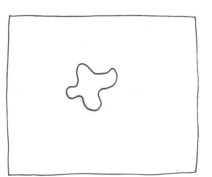

2. Approximately ½" (1 cm) away, draw a line that follows the contour edge of part of the puzzle piece. Continue the line to create another enclosed puzzle shape.

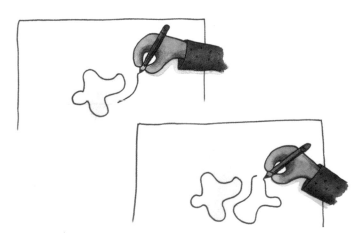

3. Continue drawing puzzle pieces that follow the curves and edges of the pieces around them as shown in the finished artwork. The pieces should radiate out from the center piece and be spaced about ½" (1 cm) apart.

4. On the color wheel (see page 60), choose a primary color. Look at the intermediate colors and secondary colors that are on either side of it. These analogous colors are the ones you will use to paint your puzzle design.

Referring to the color wheel, mix the paints as necessary to create these five colors.

5. Paint the center puzzle piece with a secondary color from the group of analogous colors you chose. Let's say you chose blue as your primary color. You could paint the center piece green as shown here.

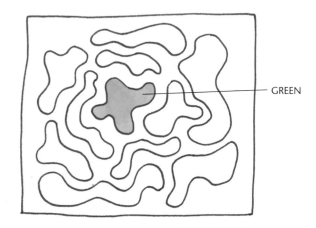

GREEN

6. Continue painting the pieces in the order your analogous color family appears on the color wheel. Paint the three puzzle pieces that surround the center piece with the appropriate intermediate color.

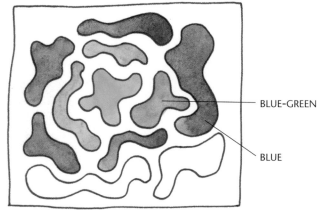

BLUE-GREEN

BLUE

7. Paint the next group of pieces with the primary color.

8. Paint the last group of pieces with the appropriate intermediate color.

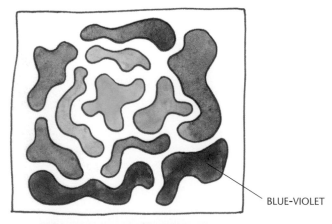

BLUE-VIOLET

9. Fill in the background with the other secondary color in your family of colors. Let dry.

10. Use the permanent black marker to go over the contour edges of your puzzle shapes to make them really stand out.

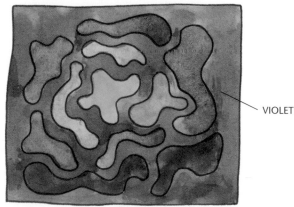

VIOLET

Value

When you work with color, as you did in the last chapter, you probably found that you occasionally needed a lighter or darker version of a certain color. In that case, you're using the design element called *value* — the lightness or darkness of a color, or of a gray.

The darkest value is pure black. The lightest value is pure white. When you use black and white next to each other, you see the greatest degree of contrast possible.

Emily, age 10

When you mix black and white together in different proportions, you create different values of grays, ranging from a very soft, pale gray to a dark steel gray.

To achieve a darker value of a color, you mix in some black. The more black you add, the darker the value. These darker colors are called *shades*.

To create lighter values, you add white. The resulting colors are called *tints*.

When you add both black and white to a color, you create a *tone*. Adding a small amount of black and white to a color "tones it down," or makes it less bright, as shown here.

Vanessa, age 8

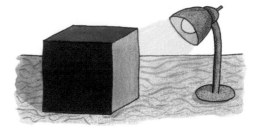

These different values of violet were created by mixing violet with black or white. See BEAUTIFUL BUTTERFLY, pages 80 to 82.

In a drawing or painting, artists use areas of light and dark values to make things look real. This technique, called *shading*, creates the look of a three-dimensional object on the flat surface of the paper or canvas.

Shading techniques vary depending on whether the object you're drawing is made up of flat surfaces, such as a box, or rounded forms, such as a cylinder or ball. You can make the angular surfaces of boxes and buildings look three-dimensional by making sharp changes in value from one side of the box to the next. The lightest value will be the surface nearest to the light source. The sides will be darker in value and the darkest surface will be the one farthest away from the light source.

To show the curving rounded surface of a form such as a cylinder or a sphere, you need to use a gradual change in value. The portion of the form facing the light will be the lightest value. As the form curves away from the light, the values gradually get darker.

To try both of these shading techniques, see WHAT'S ON THE SHELF?, pages 85 to 87, and FROM SHAPE TO FORM, pages 89 to 91.

Giant Ice Cream Cone

Creating mouthwatering scoops of your favorite ice cream flavors is as simple as using a little white paint to create light values of colors, called tints!

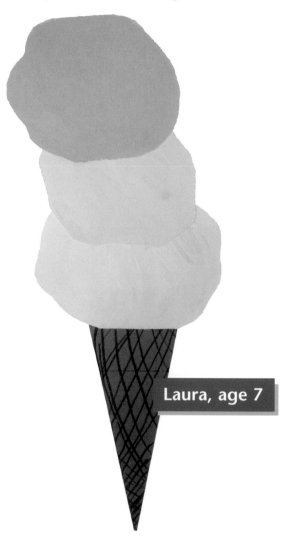

Laura, age 7

 hat you need

- ◉ Old newspaper to protect your work surface
- ◉ Scissors
- ◉ Cardboard
- ◉ Brown marker
- ◉ Small paper plates, 3
- ◉ Tempera paints in white and three primary or secondary colors (see page 59) of your choice

- ◉ Paintbrush
- ◉ Tape
- ◉ Good-quality white paper, 9" x 12" (22.5 x 30 cm), 3
- ◉ Container of water and paper towel to clean the paintbrush between colors
- ◉ Glue stick

[L]et's create it!

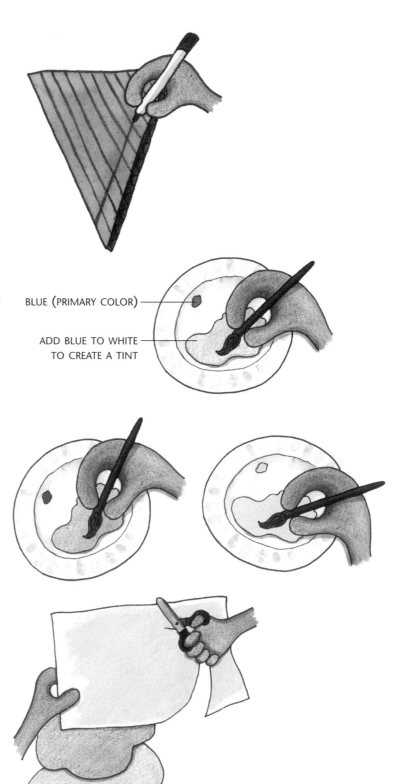

1. Cut a large narrow triangle out of the cardboard to represent a large ice cream cone. (If necessary, have an adult help you.)

2. Use the brown marker to make parallel diagonal lines on the cone. Make more diagonal lines going in the opposite direction.

3. On a paper plate, make a tint of a color to represent an ice cream flavor. To create this lighter value, add a small amount of a primary or a secondary color to a puddle of white paint and mix together.

BLUE (PRIMARY COLOR)

ADD BLUE TO WHITE TO CREATE A TINT

4. Tape the edges of one piece of white paper to the newspaper-covered work surface. Paint the paper with the paint mixture. Let dry.

5. Repeat steps 3 and 4 with two more colors of paint.

6. Cut a cloud shape out of each painted paper.

7. Glue the bottom edge of one scoop to the top edge of the cone. Glue the remaining two ice cream scoops above the one on the cone.

Beautiful Butterfly

Mix various amounts of white or black into a color to
create light and dark values (see page 76) of that color.
Paint a beautiful butterfly with this *monochromatic*
(using one color or variations of it) color scheme.

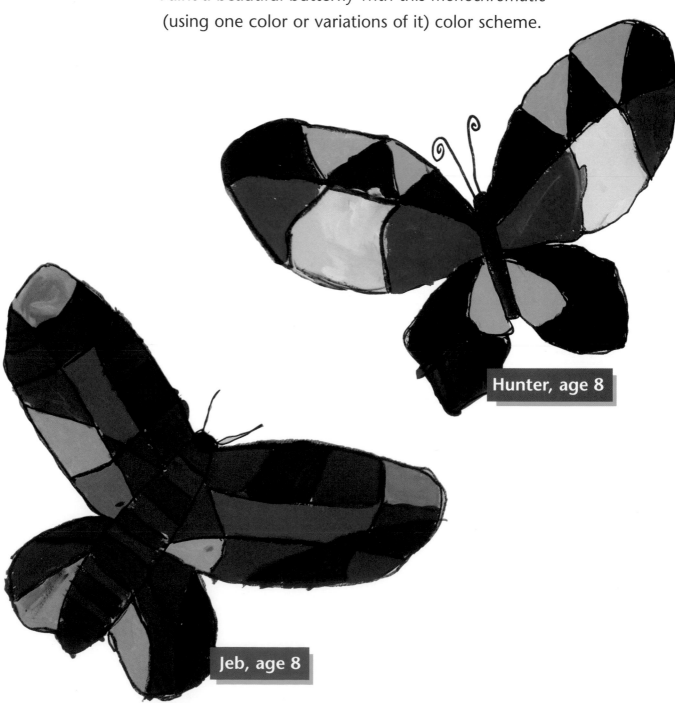

Hunter, age 8

Jeb, age 8

hat you need

- Old newspaper to protect your work surface
- Good-quality white paper, 12" x 18" (30 x 45 cm), 2
- Pencil
- Scissors
- Black permanent marker

- Tempera paints in white, black, and a primary or secondary color (see page 59) of your choice
- Paintbrush
- Container of water and paper towel to clean the paintbrush between colors
- Paper plates

Let's create it!

1. Create a symmetrical drawing (both sides match) of a butterfly. Fold one piece of paper in half. On the fold, use the pencil to draw half of a butterfly shape, large enough to almost fill the paper. Draw both a top wing and a bottom wing as shown.

   Cut out the shape. Open the paper; the butterfly will have four wings. Draw the butterfly's body in the center.

2. Use the pencil to trace around the butterfly shape onto the other piece of paper.

3. Draw three lines to divide one top wing into four sections. Make similar lines on the matching wing.

4. Make two dividing lines on one bottom wing to divide the wing into three sections. Make similar lines on the matching wing.

5. Draw over all your pencil lines with the black permanent marker.

6. Paint matching areas on either the top or the bottom wings of your butterfly with a primary or secondary color.

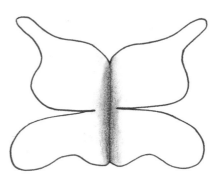

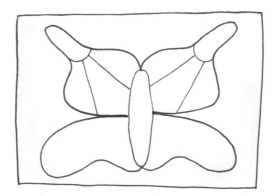

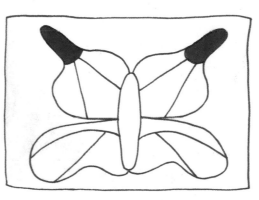

7. Paint three other matching sections with tints of that color. On the paper plate, mix a small amount of the color into a puddle of white paint. Paint one area on each matching wing with this color.

Mix a little more color into that light tint to make a darker tint. Paint two matching areas with this mixture.

Add more color to make an even darker tint. Paint two matching areas with this mixture.

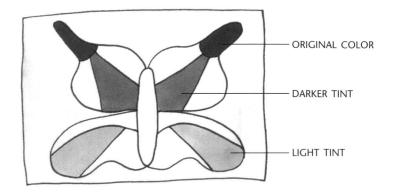

ORIGINAL COLOR

DARKER TINT

LIGHT TINT

8. Now paint three matching areas with darker shades of your color. Add a very small amount of black to a puddle of your original color. Paint a section.

Make two darker shades by adding a tiny amount of black paint each time, and paint two areas with those mixtures.

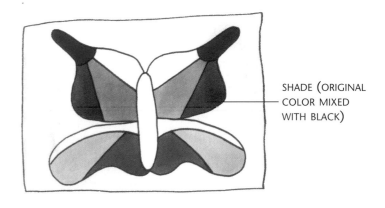

SHADE (ORIGINAL COLOR MIXED WITH BLACK)

9. Make a tone (see page 77) by mixing your original color with small amounts of both black and white. Paint the body of your butterfly with this mixture.

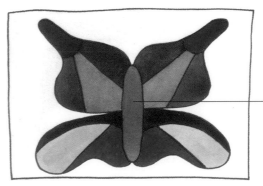

TONE (YOUR COLOR MIXED WITH BLACK AND WHITE)

Hidden Shapes

Here's a cool way to create an abstract painting (*abstract* means you are not trying to create a realistic image of something). You begin with common recognizable shapes and then break them up with the addition of a few lines. Paint these fractured shapes with different values (see page 76) of gray paint, and the recognizable shapes that you started can now also be viewed as an interesting design!

Laura, age 12

What you need

- Old newspaper to protect your work surface
- Object (to trace)
- Permanent black marker
- Good-quality white paper, 9" x 12" (22.5 x 30 cm)
- Ruler
- Tempera paints in black and white
- Paper plates, 6
- Paintbrush
- Container of water and paper towel to clean the paintbrush between colors
- Scrap paper

Let's create it!

1. Choose an object that has a interesting or attractive shape to it. Cookie cutters work well, as do simple tools like a hammer or screwdriver. Using the marker, trace around the object several times on the paper. Vary the position and angles of the object in relationship to each other and even overlap some of them to create more interest.

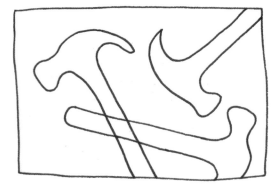

2. Use the marker and the ruler to draw five lines that are not parallel to each other. Draw three in one direction and two in the other. See how the lines divide your picture into abstract shapes?

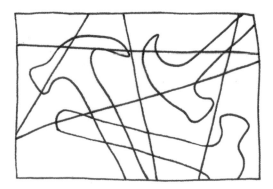

3. Create four values of gray as shown on page 76. Start with four puddles of white paint, each on a separate plate. Mix small amounts of black into each one. Test the different values on a scrap piece of paper to see if you have made mixtures that look different from each other; adjust with more paint if necessary.

4. Paint the abstract shapes with black, white, and the four shades of gray. For contrast, be sure to use different values for shapes that touch each other.

What's on the Shelf?

These objects really look as if they are sitting on the shelves!
By using shading to create light, medium, and dark values of gray
(see pages 76 and 77), you can show the angular surfaces of a shelf,
creating depth and making the shelf look three-dimensional. Positioning
each cutout picture in just the right place on the flat surface of the page
makes the items look as though they have been placed on the shelf.

Noah, age 10

What you need

- Old newspaper to protect your work surface
- Ruler
- Soft lead pencil
- White construction paper, 12" x 12" (30 x 30 cm)
- Stiff paper, 3" x 3" (7.5 x 7.5 cm)
- Scrap paper
- Scissors
- Old magazines
- Glue stick

 **et's create it!**

6" (15 CM)

1. Measure and mark 6" (15 cm) on the top and bottom edges of the larger square of paper. Use the ruler to draw a straight vertical line between the two points.

Measure and mark 6" (15 cm) along the two sides of the paper. Draw a horizontal line between those two points.

Your square is now divided into four 6" (15 cm) squares.

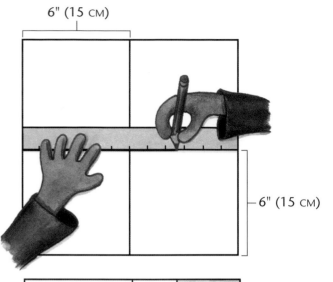

6" (15 CM)

2. Place the 3" (7.5 cm) paper square in the upper right-hand corner of one of the larger squares and trace around it.

Repeat in each of the other three squares.

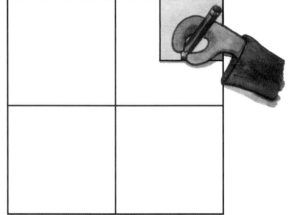

3. Make a diagonal line connecting the bottom left-hand corner of each 3" (7.5 cm) square with the bottom left-hand corner of each 6" (15 cm) square. You now have two shelves, each with two sections.

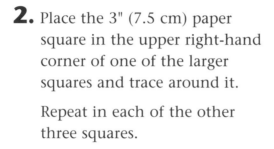 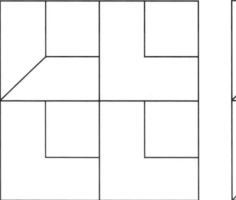 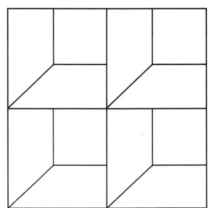

4. On the scrap paper, practice making a light, a medium, and a dark value of gray by applying different amounts of pressure on the paper with the pencil.

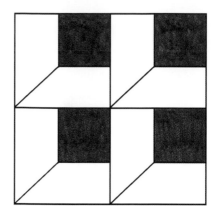

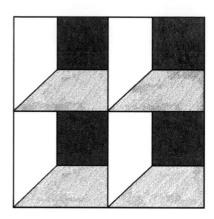

5. Shade each 3" (7.5 cm) square with a dark value of gray.

6. Shade each shape directly below those squares with a light value of gray.

7. Shade the remaining shape with a medium value of gray, as shown in the finished art on page 85. Notice how the use of values gives depth to your shelves.

8. Cut four or more pictures of objects out of magazines and glue them to your picture so the objects are sitting in each section of the shelves.

Through the Artist's Eyes

"Hands and feet are very expressive, so I often focus on them in my work. I used a charcoal pencil for this drawing because I love the rich blacks and soft blended grays I can achieve with it. The fine highlights are easily pulled out with a kneaded eraser. The strong contrast between light and dark areas and the side lighting add drama and accentuate the skin texture. My inspiration for this piece was my dance class, where I noticed many of the dancers massaging their aching feet afterward."

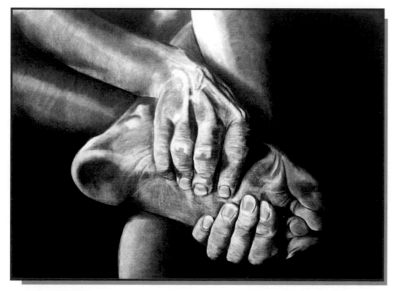

Healing Hands
Tara Belk

Meet THE *Masters*

Fernand Léger

French painter
1881–1955

Fernand Léger (fur NAWND leh ZHAY) was encouraged by his uncle to begin studying architecture at the age of 16. Upon completing his studies, he became a draftsman (the assistant who draws the early sketches for a building) for architects in Paris. At the age of 22, however, Léger began to pursue his dream of becoming an artist. He lived in a part of Paris where many other artists, such as Marc Chagall and Robert Delaunay (see page 70), also lived. They gave him encouragement as well as useful advice concerning his artwork.

   Léger's paintings, especially during the early part of his career, focused on the activity of the modern city. His style was different from the Cubist painters (see page 70) of the time, and because his paintings were full of colorful cylindrical forms and spherical shapes, the art critics jokingly referred to him as the "tubist."

Fernand Léger
*The Railway Crossing
(preliminary version)*, 1919,
oil on canvas, 54.1 x 65.7 cm
(22" x 26")
Joseph Winterbotham Collection,
gift of Mrs. Patrick Hill
in memory of Rue Winterbotham
Carpenter, 1953.341,
Photography © The Art Institute
of Chicago
© 2007 Artists Rights Society (ARS),
New York / ADAGP, Paris

From Shape to Form

▲ ▲ ▲

In *The Railway Crossing* on page 89, Fernand Léger uses vivid colors, solid and flat shapes, angles and curves, and areas of dark and light to create a sense of activity in the painting. Notice how the tubular shapes look three-dimensional. Use different color values (see pages 76 and 77) and areas of light and dark to turn flat shapes into 3-D forms just as Léger did.

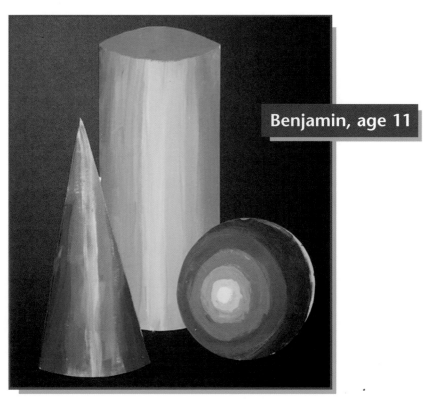

Benjamin, age 11

 hat you need

- Old newspaper to protect your work surface
- Good-quality white paper, 3
- Pencil
- Circle shape, such a glass or a small plate
- Ruler
- Tempera paints in white and three colors of your choice

- Paintbrush
- Paper plates, 3
- Container of water and paper towel to clean the paintbrush between colors
- Scissors
- Black paper, 12" x 12" (30 x 30 cm)
- Glue

1. On the white paper, draw three geometric shapes as follows:

Trace around the circle shape.

To draw a cylinder, make two parallel lines with the ruler.

Make two outward-curving lines at the top and bottom as shown. Add another line as shown to finish the top of the cylinder.

To make a large triangle shape, use the ruler to draw two straight sides. Add a slightly curved bottom line as shown.

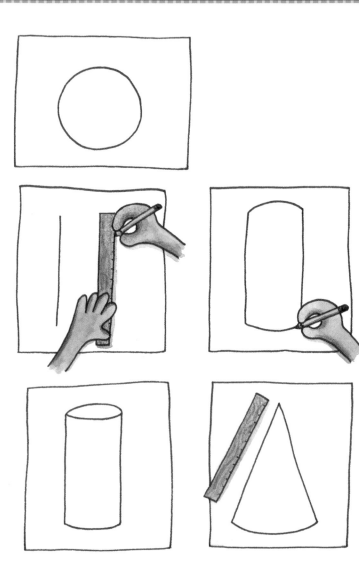

2. Choose a paint color, and use different values of it to make the circle shape look like a sphere. On a paper plate, mix a light value (a tint) by adding a small amount of your color to a puddle of white paint. Paint a small ring in the upper right portion of your circle shape.

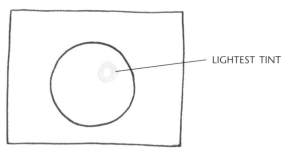

LIGHTEST TINT

3. Continue making values of this color by adding a little more of it to the paint mixture and then painting a ring of color.

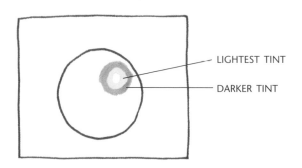

LIGHTEST TINT

DARKER TINT

4. When a complete circle of paint no longer fits inside the drawn circle, paint just the arc of the circle that does fit. Fill the circle with rings of increasingly darker tints and watch the circle shape take on the three-dimensional appearance of a sphere. Let dry.

5. Mix a light value of a new color (see step 2) and use this light tint to paint a line in the center of the cylinder shape. Don't paint the top of the cylinder.

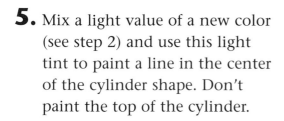

6. Make a darker tint by adding a little more color to the light value. Paint a line of this mixture on either side of the first line.

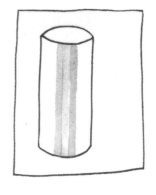

7. Continue adding a little more color to the light value and painting darker tints until your shape is filled. Paint the top of the cylinder with one of these darker tints. Let dry.

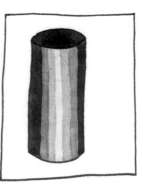

8. Mix a light value of the third color and paint a vertical line of this light tint in the center of the triangle shape. Mix and paint lines of darker and darker tints on both sides of the previous lines of color until the shape is filled. Let dry.

9. Cut out the shapes. Arrange them on the black paper, and glue them in place.

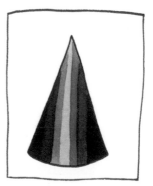

Form

Form is the element of art that describes a shape with three dimensions — height, width, and depth. Unlike a flat shape drawn on paper, you can view a form on all sides. Sometimes each view is the same and sometimes it's different. We are surrounded by forms, both natural and man-made. Just like shapes, forms are described as either *geometric* or *free-form*.

Geometric forms are precise and regular. Look back at the simple geometric shapes on page 26 and compare them to these three-dimensional forms.

CUBE   PYRAMID   CYLINDER   SPHERE   CONE

Free-form objects are irregular and uneven. The natural world is full of free-form objects — trees, rocks, clouds, and even you! Anything that has height, width, and depth and does not have a precise and regular shape is described as free-form.

Artists use form to create 3-D works of art called *sculpture in the round*, or *freestanding sculpture*. They use many different materials, including wood, metal, stone, clay, sand, glass, and paper, and different techniques.

Connie Cox used the ▶ additive process to create this sculpture vase. She modeled a vase shape from clay and gradually added more and more clay to create the facial features. To try the additive process using paper, see pages 97 to 99.

To create sculpture, artists use either the *additive process* or the *subtractive process*. The **additive process** means to add materials together to create a form.

In *Hound Dog* by Rex ▶ Inman, the finished dog sculpture looks very different from the piece of wood that it started as.

The **subtractive process** begins with a solid form, such as a piece of wood or a block of stone. The artist carves into the form, taking pieces of it away to create the form he or she wants.

The materials you use to make sculpture, such as clay for modeling or a block of vermiculite and plaster for carving, may be altogether different from those for creating two-dimensional art. Or they may just be used differently, such as bending and joining poster board in new ways to create a form. Making sculpture that has depth as well as height and width will help you when you explore the concept of space (see pages 110 to 123) and learn how to create the illusion of depth on a two-dimensional surface.

Unicorn by Louis Torres was ▶ made with sheets of steel, cut, hammered, and joined together with various gauges (thicknesses) of steel rod. Do you think the additive process or subtractive process was used to create this sculpture?

Laura, age 12

◀ This free-form sculpture was carved from a block made of plaster and vermiculite. To try a sculpture using the subtractive process, see pages 104 to 106.

Sock-Head Sculpture

This additive sculpture (see page 93) is made from mostly recycled materials. Its look changes over time as the grass-seed "hair" grows!

Spencer, age 7

Ⓦhat you need

- Old newspaper to protect your work surface
- Scissors
- Ruler
- Pair of old panty hose
- Grass seed, 1 teaspoon (5 ml)
- Peat moss
- 12" (30 cm) stick
- Yarn

- Piece of light-colored string or monofilament
- *To make facial features:* Hot-glue gun and buttons, beads, yarn, and other odds and ends
- Sand or gravel
- Empty dish detergent bottle
- Tape
- Fabric

Ⓛet's create it!

1. Cut a 12" (30 cm) section off the foot and leg portion of the panty hose.

2. Put the grass seed in the toe. Fill with peat moss. Poke the stick into the peat moss, letting several inches (cm) of the stick extend beyond the opening.

Tie closed with yarn. Turn upside down so that the stuffed portion is now the head.

3. Pinch together a small section in the middle of the stocking head as shown. Tie the string or monofilament around it to make a nose.

4. Make other facial features by gluing on buttons, beads, or other decorative items.

5. Add the sand or gravel to the bottle for weight. Insert the end of the stick into the sand or gravel to support the head.

Drape the ends of the stocking over the opening of the bottle and tape at the bottom.

6. Drape fabric over the bottle to represent clothes as shown in the finished sock head on page 94. Glue on additional details and decorations with sequins, ribbons, yarn, beads, and other materials.

Through the Artist's Eyes

"About 10 years ago, Sherry Edwards, a professor at Alabama State University, dropped a large piece of rusting metal in front of my house and challenged me to make something out of it. The material was the bottom part of a freestanding fireplace.

　　I classify myself as a 'visionary artist' because I try to see a vision of what I am about to make. Normally, the material gives me the image of what it wants to be. For two days, I studied the material and turned it around to find out what I saw in it. As I positioned the metal as the artwork now stands, I saw the vision of a 'Goddess of Fire.' That is why I have given her the name of Goddess of Fire."

Goddess of Fire
Sal Kapunan

Additive Paper Sculpture

Cut poster board into strips and shapes and connect them to make a colorful additive sculpture (see page 93). Using poster board that's a different color on each side works especially well for this paper sculpture because it adds even more visual interest.

Gabriella, age 9

What you need

- Old newspaper to protect your work surface
- Scissors
- Poster board in various colors
- Cardboard, 9" x 12" (22.5 x 30 cm)
- Glue
- Tape

Let's create it!

1. Cut several squares, rectangles, and triangles of various sizes from the poster board. Also cut some long strips. Set aside.

2. Begin building up from your cardboard base by attaching two geometric shapes to the base with the tab attachment as shown.

To make a tab attachment, bend the edge of the shape about ¼" (5 mm) at a right angle.

Put a line of glue on the bottom edge of the tab. Position this shape on your base. Secure it with tape.

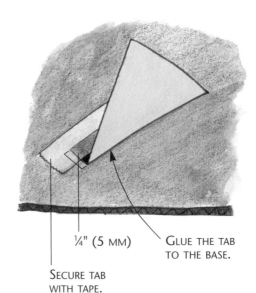

¼" (5 MM) GLUE THE TAB TO THE BASE.

SECURE TAB WITH TAPE.

3. Add another shape using a cross-slit attachment.

To make a cross-slit attachment, simply make a straight cut into your shape about ¾" (2 cm) deep. Make another ¾" (2 cm) straight cut along the top edge of the shape that is already glued to the base. Join the two pieces together, locking them in place at right angles.

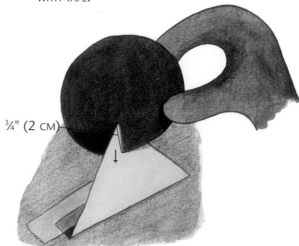

¾" (2 CM)

4. Continue adding pieces to your sculpture with either the tab attachment or the cross-slit attachment.

5. Curl or accordion-fold long strips.

Add these pieces to your sculpture using the two attachment methods.

6. Continue adding pieces to your sculpture using these different techniques until you like the way it looks from all directions.

To curl the strips, wrap them around a pencil, hold for a few seconds, and then remove.

To accordion-fold, fold the strip back and forth as shown.

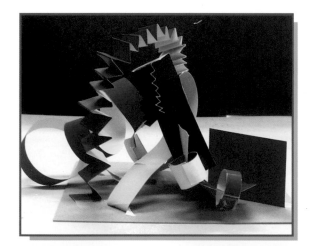

Each side of Gabriella's sculpture is a whole new piece of art!

Meet THE *Masters*

Claes Oldenburg and Coosje van Bruggen

American (Swiss-born) sculptor
1929–

Dutch sculptor
1942–

Claes (khlass) Oldenburg and Coosje van Bruggen (KOH-sha vahn BROO-gun) are two artists who began working together in 1976 to make monumental sculptures of ordinary objects. They married in 1977 and since then have created more than 40 large-scale sculptures together, many of which are displayed in major cities around the world. The colossal size of the objects allows you to see them in a new and different way. Do you think this sculpture shows how a real spoon looks to an ant?

▲ Claes Oldenburg and Coosje van Bruggen
Spoonbridge and Cherry, 1985–1988
Aluminum and stainless steel painted with polyurethane enamel
354" x 618" x 162" (9 x 15.7 x 4.1 m)
Collection Walker Art Center, Minneapolis
Gift of Frederick R. Weisman in honor of his parents, William and Mary Weisman, 1988
© Claes Oldenburg and Coosje van Bruggen

"Supersize" It!

Be inspired by the artwork of Claes Oldenburg and Coosje van Bruggen! "Supersize" a common object using papier-mâché as your art medium.

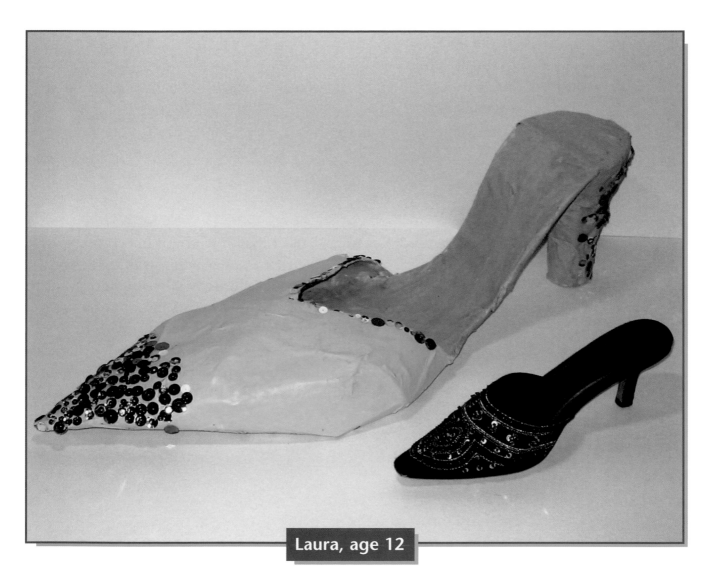

Laura, age 12

The real shoe placed next to this super-sized papier-mâché shoe gives you an idea of the sculpture's large size.

What you need

- Old newspapers to protect your work surface and for the papier-mâché
- Materials for the supporting form: cardboard, poster board, balloons, newspaper, and masking tape
- Scissors
- Ruler
- White glue
- Measuring cup
- Mixing bowl
- Tempera paints
- Paintbrush
- Container of water and paper towels to clean the paintbrush between colors
- Decorative items (optional)

Let's create it!

1. Decide on an ordinary small object that you would like to make extra large. Think of something that has personal meaning to you. For instance, if strawberries are your favorite fruit, you might want to make a colossal strawberry. Or, if you are a sports fan, how about a giant football or soccer ball?

2. Make a supporting form to show the shape of the object you want to make. You can use cardboard boxes and tubes, balloons, wadded newspaper, or other scrap materials. Hold all of the parts together with masking tape. The form for the large shoe on page 101, for example, was made out of corrugated cardboard, poster board, paper-towel tubes, paper towels, and tape.

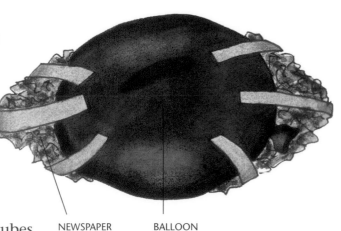

NEWSPAPER   BALLOON

3. Cut strips of newspaper approximately 1" to 2" (2.5 to 5 cm) wide and 4" to 6" (10 to 15 cm) long.

Mix two parts glue with one part water in the mixing bowl.

4. Dip a newspaper strip into the glue-water mixture, then pull it between your fingers to remove the excess paste.

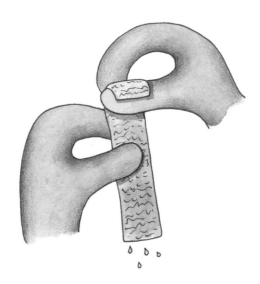

5. Apply the glue-covered strip to your support form. Use wide strips in large areas and smaller strips when turning corners. Overlap strips for extra strength.

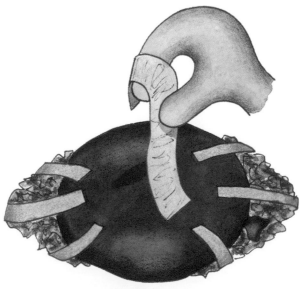

6. Apply two or three layers of strips, smoothing over all the rough edges as you go. Let the form dry completely between layers.

7. Paint your sculpture. Add textural decorations for effect, if you like.

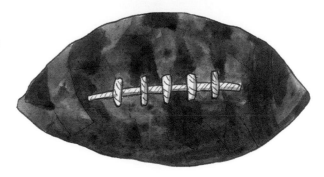

"Take Away" Sculpture

The word *sculpt* originally meant to "carve in stone." The Greeks and Romans made most of their sculptures with this method. Carving is a sculpting technique where the artist cuts or chips away the material. A mix of plaster of paris, vermiculite, and water hardens into a block that's easily shaped with a blunt knife. It will give you a feel for the *subtractive process* (see page 93) for creating sculpture.

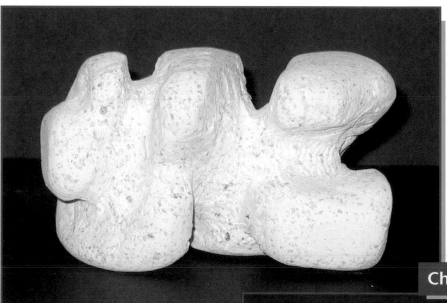

A 3-D sculpture can be seen from various sides and angles, offering different points of view.

Chelsea, age 13

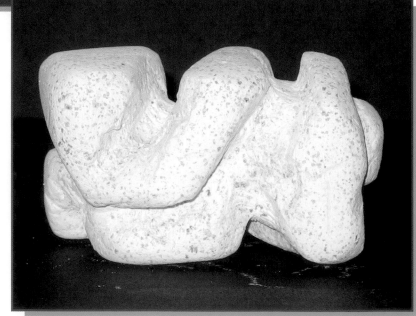

What you need

- Spoon
- Measuring cup
- Plaster of Paris
- Water
- Vermiculite
- Mixing bowl
- Clean empty waxed-cardboard container, such as a small cream or milk container
- Table knife (with adult permission)
- Sandpaper

Let's create it!

1. Mix three parts plaster of Paris, three parts water, and two parts vermiculite together in the bowl. Open the top of the container. Pour in the mixture and let harden for 24 hours.

2. Peel away the container to reveal a solid rectangular form.

3. Think about the form you want your sculpture to take. Will you make a recognizable object or a free-form sculpture? Use the table knife to begin carving away what is not part of your sculpture idea.

4. Turn your sculpture as you work so that you carve all four sides, creating different points of view for the viewer.

5. Use the sandpaper to smooth any rough areas.

Through the Artist's Eyes

"I've been carving wooden figures like these for 10 years. I like creating a detailed animal shape, complete with fur and facial features, from a solid block of wood. I start with a large log and use a chain saw to block out an outline of the piece by cutting triangles, squares, and other shapes. After this main 'block out' is finished, I use a smaller saw to add detail to the carving."

Bear Sculpture
Dallas Smart

Dancing Mobile

▲▲▲

A mobile is a sculpture made up of parts that are delicately balanced so that the slightest air current sets them moving, changing the sculpture's appearance. You can view this type of sculpture from different angles while standing in one place! Alexander Calder, the artist considered responsible for the invention of the mobile, said, "It is my feeling that art is too static to reflect our world of movement." *Static* describes something that barely changes, or shows little movement or animation. Do you agree with Calder?

Laura, age 12

What you need

- Scissors
- Poster board or foam sheets (available at art supply stores)
- Glue
- Decorations (optional)
- Hole punch
- Yarn
- Plastic straws (one straw for every two shapes you make)

Let's create it!

1. Cut five to seven geometric or free-form shapes from the poster board or foam sheets.

2. Decorate both sides of each shape by cutting out a smaller shape from another color and gluing it on. Add other decorations if you like.

3. Use the hole punch to make a hole near the top of each shape. Set the shapes aside.

4. For each shape, cut a piece of yarn 10" (25 cm) long. Fold each piece in half and tie the ends together. Thread the ends of the yarn through the hole in each shape and back through the loop as shown.

Make several more yarn loops and set them aside.

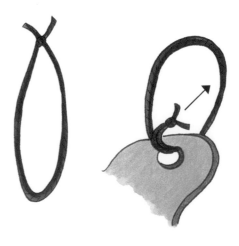

5. Cut slits ¼" (5 mm) long at both ends of the straws. Hang a shape at each end of one straw by slipping the knotted end of the string into the slit.

6. Loop a knotted string around the midpoint of the straw with the two shapes. Adjust the yarn to make the straw balance.

7. Add a shape to one end of another straw. Slip the support string from the previous section into the slit of the other end of the new straw.

8. Add a support string around the midpoint of the new straw. Adjust to find the balance point.

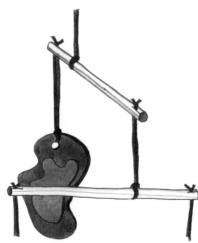

9. Repeat steps 7 and 8 to add more sections to your mobile and balance them.

10. Add one final support string to the top straw so you can hang your mobile from the ceiling and watch it change position and turn.

Space

When you think of *space* as the area all around a object — above, below, behind, and even within — you can see that it's an important design element. Knowing how to work with space in a drawing or painting comes in very handy when you want to reproduce something — a scene in nature or a three-dimensional object, for example — and have it look realistic.

Sculptors work with forms that take up actual physical space (see pages 92 to 109). Other artists, such as painters or illustrators, use certain techniques to create the illusion of physical space in flat, two-dimensional artwork. They begin by thinking about their flat drawing or painting surface as three separate areas: *background*, *middle ground*, and *foreground*.

VANISHING
POINT

BACKGROUND

MIDDLE GROUND

FOREGROUND

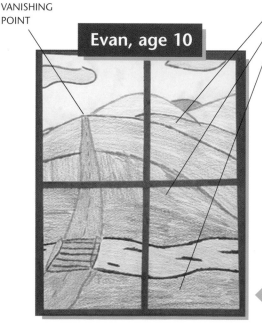

Evan, age 10

To show distance and depth on the flat surface, artists then apply the following six techniques of *perspective* to those three areas.

Line. *One-point perspective* is a mathematical approach to showing depth in a two-dimensional piece of art. All lines that move away from the viewer into the distance meet at one point on the horizon line, called the *vanishing point*. This technique can be applied to the sides of buildings or the flat shape of a road, for example.

To try creating the illusion of space in your artwork, see VIEW FROM THE WINDOW, pages 121 to 123.

LINE

COLOR

PLACEMENT

OVERLAP

DETAIL

SIZE

▲ In this watercolor landscape painting by Richard Kaiser, the artist applied the techniques of perspective to create both distance and depth in his artwork. The painting is two-dimensional, but it looks as though you could step right into it.

Placement. Objects in the foreground appear to be closer to the viewer. Objects placed in the background seem farther away. See how the red house and barn in the foreground of the painting seem closer than the white house in the distance?

Overlap. When one object covers part of another, the object in front appears to be closer to the viewer than the one in back. Notice the big tree that covers part of the white house.

Size. Large objects seem to be closer to the viewer than small objects. The fence posts beginning at the lower left corner of the picture get smaller as they move into the distance. Artists can also indicate the size of an object by placing it next to another object in correct proportion and scale. How do you know that the silo is tall?

Color. Brightly colored objects appear closer to the viewer than objects with light, pale colors. Notice that the hills and mountains closest to the viewer are darker in color.

Detail. Objects that have sharp outlines and lots of detail seem to be closer to the viewer than objects with fuzzy edges and little detail. The artist showed much more detail in the houses closer to the viewer than on the house in the distance.

Meet the Masters

René Magritte

Belgian painter
1898–1967

Sometimes an artist will use proportion or scale (see page 115) in an exaggerated way. In this picture, an apple fills the entire room. The artist René Magritte has exaggerated the size, or scale, of the apple to create a dreamlike world. Do you think that the painting would be as interesting if he had painted the apple in correct proportion to the room?

Magritte's main objective in his paintings was to show real space as well as a striking illusion. He painted everyday objects in unusual ways, often changing the size to make something appear bigger or smaller than in the real world. Or he would combine two easily recognizable images to create a magical image. For an intriguing example of this, visit the website of the Museum of Modern Art (see RESOURCES, page 124) to see his painting of an eye filled with a cloudy sky, called *The False Mirror*.

René Magritte is an example of a *surrealist* painter. In French, *sur* means "beyond." Surrealism is a type of art that is "beyond reality." Do you think this term is a good description of Magritte's paintings?

▲ René Magritte
The Listening Room, 1952
oil on canvas
18" x 22" (45 x 55 cm)
The Menil Collection, Houston, gift of Fariha Friedrich
© 2007 C. Herscovici, Brussels / Artists Rights Society (ARS), New York

Giant Sunflower

Proportion and scale help us understand how much space an object takes up. When things are in correct proportion to each other, you get an idea of their true sizes. Sunflowers by nature can grow to be up to 6 feet (1.8 m) tall. Imagine, however, that you grew a prizewinning sunflower that was *18 feet (5.5 m)* tall! Play with the concept of scale to create a surrealist drawing in the style of René Magritte to show how you would look standing next to this huge sunflower.

Andrew, age 8

What you need

- Real sunflower (as a model) or picture of one from a seed catalog
- Pencil
- Good-quality paper, 12" x 18" (30 x 45 cm)
- Crayons

Let's create it!

1. Observe the sunflower and notice the pattern of seeds in the center of the blossom. Also take note of the size, shape, and color of the petals that surround the center.

2. Draw a horizon line about 3" (7.5 cm) from the bottom of the page. Draw the sunflower at the top of the page.

3. Make a stem that extends from the flower to the ground area. Make sure the flower is growing from the ground and not sitting on the horizon line. Add a leaf or two to the stem.

4. Draw yourself standing next to the giant sunflower. Think about what size you will draw yourself to show that the sunflower is very, very big.

5. Color the sunflower and yourself. Don't forget to color the background.

Creating a Sense of Scale

When one object is compared to another and both objects are *true to scale* (shown at their proper size), you get a visual clue of what size they both are.

With author Sandi Henry's daughters Lydia and Laura posing next to this snowman, you can tell it's a really big one! ▶

Harvest-Time Perspective Collage

This collage of vegetables uses the perspective techniques of placement and overlap (see pages 110 and 111) to show depth. Which techniques make the objects look closer and which make them look farther away?

Colleen, age 10

What you need

- Old newspaper to protect your work surface
- Vegetables in various sizes and colors (either actual vegetables or pictures from seed catalogs)
- Scissors
- Construction paper in various colors, 9" x 12" (22.5 x 30 cm)
- Glue
- Light-colored construction paper, 6" x 18" (15 x 45 cm)
- Black construction paper, 12" x 18" (30 x 45 cm)

[L]et's create it!

1. Look closely at the shape of each vegetable and cut the shapes out of the appropriate-colored construction paper. For certain vegetables, you may want to make more than one cutout. Set aside.

2. Glue the 6" x 18" (15 x 45 cm) piece of construction paper to the bottom of the black piece. The light-colored piece represents a table to hold the vegetables.

3. To arrange the vegetables on the page, begin with the shapes that you want to have appear farther away, placing them closer to the top edge of the table.

4. Add more fruits and vegetable shapes closer to the bottom edge of the page. Overlap some of the ones you added in step 3 to represent that these additional shapes are in front of the others.

BACKGROUND

FOREGROUND

5. Once you are happy with the arrangement of your composition, glue the shapes in place.

3-D Shapes

Want to draw shapes that seem to jump right off the page? To make two-dimensional artwork look three-dimensional, artists use one-point perspective (see page 110), where all the lines move back into space and meet at a single point in the picture. In this activity, you'll see how one-point perspective will help you draw shapes that seem to move right toward the viewer.

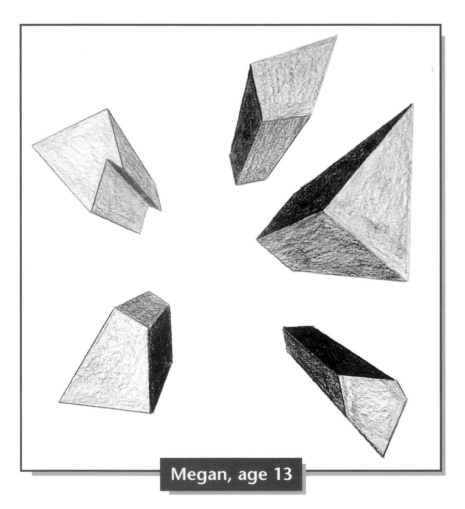

Megan, age 13

What you need

- ☙ Pencil
- ☙ Good-quality drawing paper, 12" x 18" (30 x 45 cm)
- ☙ Ruler
- ☙ Colored pencils

L et's create it!

1. Make a dot near the center of your paper. This will be your vanishing point (the point where things seem to be drawn away from the viewer into deep space).

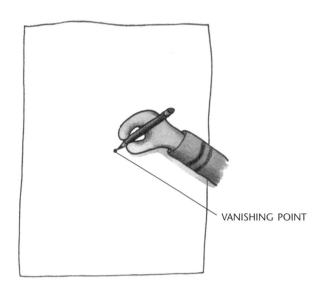

VANISHING POINT

2. Using the ruler, draw five to seven geometric shapes in the space around the vanishing point.

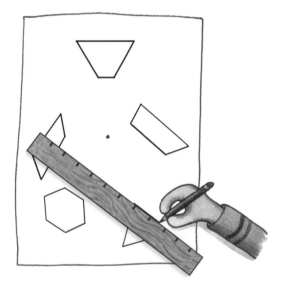

3. Make your shapes look three-dimensional by showing their sides, creating the look of their physical form. To do this, lightly draw a line from every corner of every shape that can connect to the vanishing point without "cutting through" the shape.

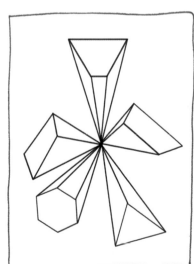

4. Decide how deep you want each shape to be, then draw the back edge. These lines will be parallel to the original shape that you drew in step 2.

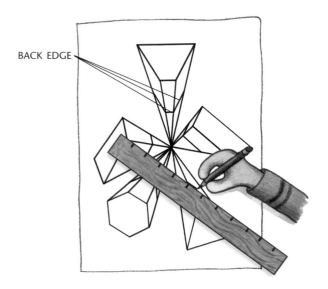

BACK EDGE

5. Erase the lines that extend beyond the edges of the form to the vanishing point.

6. To add extra dimension to your picture, apply shading with the colored pencils to create light and dark values (see pages 76 and 77). To place the different values appropriately, imagine that you are holding the light source and visualize that as the shapes recede into deep space, they are moving away from the light. Use the lightest value on the surfaces nearest the light source, and the darkest value on the one farthest away.

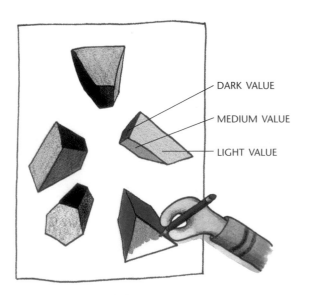

DARK VALUE

MEDIUM VALUE

LIGHT VALUE

View from the Window

Whenever you look out a window, you see a view. You might see trees, fields, animals, sky, clouds, or shops and buildings. These views are called *landscapes*. Using the techniques of perspective (see pages 110 and 111), draw a landscape view that recedes into the distance. Then create the look of a window with the addition of a few construction-paper strips. Your scene might be what you see out of a window in your house — or an imaginary scene of what you would like to see!

Emily, age 10

What you need

- Old newspaper to protect your work surface
- Good-quality white paper, 9" x 12" (22.5 x 30 cm)
- Ruler (optional)
- Pencil
- Crayons, colored pencils, or markers
- Scissors
- Light brown construction paper
- Glue

Let's create it!

1. With the white paper positioned vertically, lightly draw three lines at different levels to represent the foreground, middle ground and background.

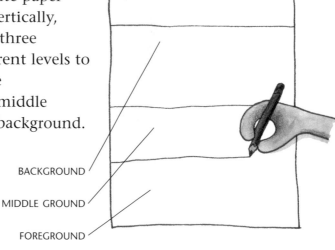

BACKGROUND

MIDDLE GROUND

FOREGROUND

2. Start by sketching the objects that are closest to the window. To make them appear closer to the viewer, make them larger with more details, and use bolder colors. Draw these shapes near the bottom of the page.

3. Sketch smaller shapes placed higher on the page to show things that are in the middle ground and the background. These shapes will have less details and lighter colors.

4. Color your picture with crayons, colored pencils, or markers.

5. Cut the light brown construction paper into ¼" (5 mm) strips and glue on as crosspieces to suggest window panes.

Cut 1" (2.5 cm) strips and glue around the outside edges of the picture to frame the window.

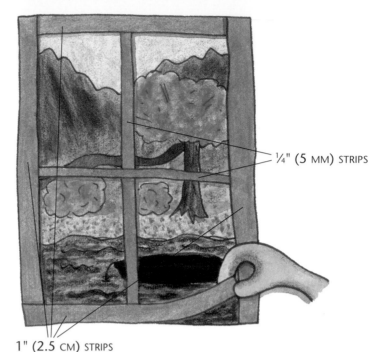

¼" (5 MM) STRIPS

1" (2.5 CM) STRIPS

Through the Artist's Eyes

Stabler-Leadbeater Apothecary Shop
Joe Miller

"This scene is from America's oldest drugstore in Alexandria, Virginia. Martha Washington and General Robert E. Lee were regular customers here. This painting was commissioned, and copies of it were sold to support the store, which is now a museum.

The painting has depth perspective because the Capitol building [in Washington, DC] seen in the background through the window is smaller than the bottles and books in the foreground inside the pharmacy. Another technique for creating perspective is the use of hard edges and detail. There is more detail in the foreground items; the viewer can see some of the pharmacy labels. The background, on the other hand, was kept soft."

Resources

Viewing Art Online

Here are the Web addresses for the museums referred to in MEET THE MASTERS! Search for an image using either an artist's name or the name of the work of art.

The Albertina, Vienna, Austria, www.albertina.at

The Art Institute of Chicago, Chicago, IL www.artic.edu

The Menil Collection, Houston, TX, www.menil.org

Metropolitan Museum of Art, New York, NY www.metmuseum.org

Museum of Modern Art, New York, NY www.moma.org

Solomon R. Guggenheim Museum, New York, NY www.guggenheim.org/new_york_index.shtml

Walker Art Center, Minneapolis, MN www.walkerart.org

Art Supplies

Cheap Joe's Art Stuff
374 Industrial Park Drive
Boone, NC 28607
800-227-2788
www.cheapjoes.com

Dick Blick Art Materials
P.O. Box 1267
Galesburg, IL 61402-1267
800-828-4648
www.dickblick.com

Sax Arts & Crafts
2725 South Moorland Road
New Berlin, WI 53151
800-558-6696
www.saxarts.com

Index

Index (cont.)

MORE GOOD CHILDREN'S BOOKS FROM
williamsonbooks™

Williamson Books are available from your bookseller or directly from Ideals Publications. Please see last page for ordering information or to visit our website.

More Award-Winning Books ★ by Sandi Henry ★

Parents' Choice Recommended
USING COLOR IN YOUR ART!
Choosing Colors for Impact & Pizzazz

Parents' Choice Recommended
Orbus Pictus Award for Outstanding Nonfiction
KIDS' ART WORKS!
Creating with Color, Design, Texture & More

Teachers' Choice Award
Dr. Toy Best Vacation Product
CUT-PAPER PLAY!
Dazzling Creations from Construction Paper

Parents' Choice Gold Award
American Bookseller Pick of the Lists
THE KIDS' MULTICULTURAL ART BOOK
Art & Craft Experiences from Around the World
BY ALEXANDRA M. TERZIAN

American Bookseller Pick of the Lists
Skipping Stones Nature & Ecology Honor Award
ECOART!
Earth-Friendly Art & Craft Experiences
for 3- to 9-Year-Olds
BY LAURIE CARLSON

American Bookseller Pick of the Lists
Dr. Toy Best Vacation Product
KIDS' CRAZY ART CONCOCTIONS
50 Mysterious Mixtures for Art & Craft Fun
BY JILL FRANKEL HAUSER

American Bookseller Pick of the Lists
Parents' Choice Recommended
ADVENTURES IN ART
Arts & Crafts Experiences for
8- to 13-Year-Olds
BY SUSAN MILORD

ForeWord Magazine Book of the Year Silver Award
THE KIDS' BOOK OF INCREDIBLY FUN CRAFTS
BY ROBERTA GOULD

LIGHTHOUSES OF NORTH AMERICA!
Exploring Their History, Lore & Science
BY LISA TRUMBAUER

SUPER SCIENCE CONCOCTIONS
50 Mysterious Mixtures for Fabulous Fun
BY JILL FRANKEL HAUSER

KIDS CARE!
75 Ways to Make a Difference for
People, Animals & the Environment
BY REBECCA OLIEN

TALES ALIVE!
Ten Multicultural Folktales with Activities
BY SUSAN MILORD

BECOMING THE BEST YOU CAN BE!
Developing 5 Traits You Need
to Achieve Your Personal Best
BY JILL FRANKEL HAUSER

AWESOME OCEAN SCIENCE
Investigating the Secrets of
the Underwater World
BY CINDY A. LITTLEFIELD

WORDPLAY CAFÉ
Cool Codes, Priceless Puzzles
& Phantastic Phonetic Phun
BY MICHAEL KLINE

KIDS WRITE!
Fantasy & Sci Fi, Mystery,
Autobiography, Adventure & More
BY REBECCA OLIEN

GREAT GAMES!
Ball, Board, Quiz & Word,
Indoors & Out, for Many or Few!
BY SAM TAGGAR WITH SUSAN WILLIAMSON

KIDS MAKE MAGIC
The complete Guide to
Becoming an Amazing Magician
BY RON BURGESS

Learning Magazine Teachers' Choice Award
KIDS' EASY-TO-CREATE
WILDLIFE HABITATS
For Small Spaces in City, Suburb, Countryside
BY EMILY STETSON

Parents' Choice Gold Award
Dr. Toy Best Vacation Product
THE KIDS' NATURE BOOK
365 Indoor/Outdoor Activities & Experiences
BY SUSAN MILORD

ForeWord Magazine Book of the Year Gold Award
THE SECRET LIFE OF MATH
Discover How (and Why) Numbers Have
Survived from the Cave Dwellers to Us!
BY ANN MCCALLUM

American Bookseller Pick of the Lists
Benjamin Franklin Best Education/Teaching Award
American Institute of Physics Science Writing Award
Parents' Choice Honor Award
GIZMOS & GADGETS
Creating Science Contraptions
that Work (& Knowing Why)
BY JILL FRANKEL HAUSER

Learning Magazine Teachers' Choice Award
GEOLOGY ROCKS!
50 Hands-on Activities to Explore the Earth
BY CINDY BLOBAUM

ForeWord Magazine Book of the Year Finalist
SKYSCRAPERS!
Super Structures to Design & Build
BY CAROL A. JOHMANN

Parents' Choice Recommended
BRIDGES!
Amazing Structures to Design, Build & Test
BY CAROL A. JOHMANN & ELIZABETH J. REITH

Parents' Choice Silver Honor Award
ANCIENT ROME!
Exploring the Culture, People
& Ideas of this Powerful Empire
BY AVERY HART & SANDRA GALLAGHER

Visit Our Website! To see what's new with Williamson Books and Ideals Publications and learn more about specific titles, visit our website at:

www.idealsbooks.com

To Order Books:

You'll find Williamson Books at your favorite bookstore or you can order directly from Ideals Publications. We accept Visa and MasterCard (please include the number and expiration date).

Order on our secure website:
www.idealsbooks.com

Toll-free phone orders with credit cards:
1-800-586-2572

Toll-free fax orders:
1-888-815-2759

Or send a check with your order to:
Ideals Publications
Williamson Books Orders
535 Metroplex Drive, Suite 250
Nashville, Tennessee 37211

Catalog request: web, mail, or phone

Please add **$4.00** for postage for one book plus **$1.00** for each additional book. Satisfaction is guaranteed or full refund without questions or quibbles.